The Jesus Moses Knew

How to See Christ

in the Old Testament

by Vicki Huffman

Copyright © 2017 by Vicki Huffman
First printing 2017 in the United States of America.
ISBN-13-978-1546607618
ISBN-10 1546607617

Cover design by Rosalie Sherwood, DesignerType.com

All rights reserved. No portion of this book may be used or reproduced by any means, graphic, electronic, or mechanical, including photocopying, recording, taping or by any information storage retrieval system without the written permission of the author, except in the case of brief quotations embodied in articles and reviews.

Vicki Huffman is the author of four other books including: *The Best of Times* (originally published by Broadman Press); *Plus Living: Looking for Joy in All the Right Places* (originally published by Harold Shaw Publishers); *Still Looking: Finding the Peace of God in Job Loss*; and *A Secret Hope* (a novel), all republished and available through ***amazon.com*** in print and e-book. You may contact the author by email at: vickiwrites@aol.com.

All scripture quotations, unless otherwise indicated, are taken from the Holy Bible, New International Version®, NIV®. Copyright © 1973, 1978, 1984, 2011 by Biblica, Inc.™ Used by permission of

Zondervan. All rights reserved worldwide. www.zondervan.com The "NIV" and "New International Version" are trademarks registered in the United States Patent and Trademark Office by Biblica, Inc.™

Scripture quotations marked (NKJV) are taken from the New King James Version®. Copyright © 1982 by Thomas Nelson. Used by permission. All rights reserved.

Scripture quotations marked (ESV) are from The Holy Bible, English Standard Version® (ESV®), copyright © 2001 by Crossway, a publishing ministry of Good News Publishers. Used by permission. All rights reserved.

Scripture quotations from THE MESSAGE: Copyright © by Eugene H. Peterson 1993, 1994, 1995, 1996, 2000, 2001, 2002. Used by permission of Tyndale House Publishers, Inc.

CONTENTS

Foreword
Acknowledgements
Here, There, and Everywhere

PART I BEGINNING WITH MOSES

1 Last (and Not-So-Last) Words
    Last Words
    Not-So-Last Words
    Look Deeply, See Clearly
    Theo—what?
    Prophetically Speaking

2 The Jesus Moses Knew
    Beginning with Moses
    The Creator: Genesis 1–2
    He Walks with Me: Genesis 3
    The Serpent-Crusher: Genesis 3
    Abel, a Type of Christ: Genesis 4
    Enoch Walked with God: Genesis 5

3 A Broken World
    The Ark and Our Security in Christ: Genesis 6–8
    The Semitic Line of Christ: Genesis 9
    And God Came Down: Genesis 11
    A Broken Man: Job

4 Abraham's Day
    Abraham and His Seed: Genesis 12
    Melchizedek, a Type of Christ: Genesis 14
    The Lord Who Sees Me: Genesis 16
    The Lord Visits Abraham: Genesis 17

5 The Jesus Abraham Knew
     The Lord Who Came to Dinner: Genesis 18
     Abraham's Request: Genesis 18
     A Promise Is a Promise
     Abraham's Promised son and God's Promised Son
     A Type of Christ's Sacrifice: Genesis 22

6 Isaac, the Quiet Man
     Isaac, the Bridegroom: Genesis 24
     More than One Type

7 Jacob, God's Struggler
     Jacob, the Schemer: Genesis 25–28
     Jacob, the Wrestler: Genesis 32
     Jacob, the Prophet: Genesis 49

8 Joseph, from the Pit to the Palace
     Joseph, a Type of Christ as Savior: Genesis 37–50
     The Tables Turn: Genesis 42–45

9 Moses, the savior and Jesus, the Savior
     Types and Shadows
     Like a Lamb: Exodus 12
     In the Cloud and Fire: Exodus 13
     Between the Devil and the Deep Red Sea: Exodus 14
     Their Daily Manna: Exodus 16

10 Moses and the Lawbreakers
     Water from the Rock: Exodus 17
     The Bronze Snake: Numbers 21
     A Place of Refuge: Numbers 35
     Glimpses of Grace

11 Christ in the Tabernacle and the Offerings
    The House that God Built
    Christ in the Tabernacle: Exodus 25—30
    Christ in the Offerings: Leviticus
    Christ, the Coming Prophet: Deuteronomy 18

PART II HIS STORY IN HISTORY

12 The Jesus Joshua Knew
    Detoured
    Joshua Takes the Lead
    Judging Israel
    Boaz and Christ, Kinsman-Redeemers

13 Making History
    The Best Teacher
    Samuel, Kings & Chronicles
    David, a Royal Learning Curve
    The Jesus Elijah Knew
    There and Back Again

14 The Jesus David Knew
    Not Hid from Our Eyes
    The Jesus David Sang About
    The House and Lineage of David
    David's son and the Son of David

PART III THE JESUS THE PROPHETS KNEW

15 The Suffering Savior Isaiah Knew
    When Isaiah Saw the Lord
    An Unconventional Arrival
    His Coming Announced
    The Suffering Servant: Isaiah 53
    The Shepherd and the Lamb
    And Many More

16 The Reigning Savior Daniel Knew
    What Happens Next?
    What Daniel Saw
    Zechariah's Coming King
    Malachi: The Sun Also Rises
    His Coming Unannounced
    And Many More

17 The Jesus We Know
    To Know Him
    Without a Doubt

Sources

Foreword

Vicki Huffman is a gifted writer. She is a wife, mother, grandmother, Bible teacher, and friend to many. For several years it has been my privilege to co-teach a senior adult Bible Class with her. I admire her knowledge of Scripture as well as her ability to expound the Scripture and illustrate with life's experiences.

Vicki clears up the misconception many hold today that the Old Testament is *only* a history book. *The Jesus Moses Knew* brings Christ front and center in the Old Testament. This book makes it abundantly clear that the plan of God for mankind's salvation began even before the world was created (Ephesians 1:4). Throughout the Old Testament, mankind must decide what to do with the reality of a sovereign Lord and a coming Messiah.

The Old Testament is a book of history: *His story*! It is a historic record of God's salvation extended to mankind through obedience and faith. The Old and New Testaments are a continuum of events that declare the reality of God's love and grace for mankind.

This book is an excellent resource for finding the many likenesses of Christ in the Old Testament. It reads like a novel, and it only takes a sample reading for one to become fully engrossed in *The Jesus Moses Knew*. This book will give you a greater understanding of the Old Testament that God intends for His people to know. I believe nothing is more timely, or more needful, than the subject addressed in this book. The crying need of the church today is for discernment— the ability to recognize truth and distinguish it from error. Vicki Huffman does this so well.

Ken R. Speakman
The Gideons International
Director International Division, Ret.

Acknowledgments

No book is created without the help of others. So I'm grateful to recognize those who have helped me during this process:

To my husband, Richard Huffman and my daughter, Christa Young, I appreciate you're being excellent first readers and proofers.

To my son, Dr. Cole Huffman, Senior Pastor of First Evangelical in Memphis. Thank you for being a ready source for questions. (You're like a doctrinal Google!)

To Ken Speakman, thank you for all your help and encouragement and for writing the Foreword. I admire your love for people and your dedication to the study and spread of the Word.

To Rosalie Sherwood, a designer I had the pleasure to work with at two publishing houses. Thank you for your great cover design.

To the members of my class on Christ in the Old Testament and the members of the Friendship Sunday School class at Tulip Grove Baptist Church. You were the original guinea pigs for much of this material, and I appreciate your love of the Word.

Here, There, and Everywhere

Until I was five, I lived with my grandparents in a little town (about a thousand people) that had no kindergarten. My grandmother, with only a sixth-grade education herself, taught me what she *thought* I needed to know before entering first grade: how to read and write. She succeeded, but this made for several "Vicki is bored" report cards in first and second grade.

Grandma was a woman of deep faith who made sure I had a set of Bible story books which she and I read cover to cover several times. For many years I thought that *was* the Bible—just a more expanded version (five volumes!) with colorful pictures. But in my early twenties, I started going to Bible classes. There I discovered that the Bible is much more than stories and ancient history: it is *His story.* And I was shocked to find out that Jesus is in *all* of it. Even in the Old Testament, long before the baby Jesus made an appearance in Bethlehem! That knowledge—which blossomed into a spiritual awakening and my conversion to Christianity—began a lifetime of Bible study, finding out *what else* I'd never known about Jesus.

As many others have said, in Bible study we never know or learn it all. In any passage, no matter how familiar, we can find new things. That's especially true in the Old Testament because Christians, in this age after the cross, have a tendency not to give much attention to it. Possibly we got bogged down the first or second time we tried to read through Leviticus or Ezekiel and decided to wade in less deep theological waters. (I did for many years.)

But sometimes our avoidance is more rationalized. Maybe we think that the Old Testament is "Jewish" and the New Testament is "Christian." Or that we are supposed to be loyal to the New Testament only. Perhaps we even think the New Testament *replaced* the Old Testament (rather than *fulfilled* it).

With these misconceptions rattling around in our minds and churches, it's no wonder many Christians have a limited understanding of what the Old Testament contains. Or that we're sometimes visibly uncomfortable when the lesson or sermon topic is in one of those more obscure sections. You know what I mean. You suddenly realize the pages in that section of your not-brand-new Bible have never been pulled apart, and you try to separate them quietly without anyone noticing.

An old couplet by St. Augustine explains in a pithy way the true cooperative relationship between the Old and New Testaments:

*"The New is in the Old concealed:
the Old is by the New revealed."*

This book is about some of what is concealed in the Old and revealed in the New.

All You Can Eat
If you've ever gone to a buffet at a restaurant or a "dinner on the ground" at a country church, you know something about abundance. And talk about variety! You put little portions of many things on that quickly-shrinking plate. But sometimes, before making it to the groaning dessert table, you're saying, "My eyes were bigger than my stomach."

I felt a little like that writing this book. I knew there were so many wonderful examples of Christ in the Old Testament that it would be hard to choose some and leave others. And it was. But my goal is not for this to be an exhaustive book—or to exhaust you as you read it. I want to share with you a number of eye-opening things I've learned about Christ. These have increased my knowledge of Him but, more importantly, have deepened my love for Him and helped me better understand His love for me. And that understanding has brought me great peace and joy.

Think of this book as a buffet as to its spiritual nutritional value. That's not such a stretch because the Bible describes some of its contents as food. Peter told believers, "Like newborn babies, crave pure spiritual milk, so that by it you may grow up in your salvation, now that you have tasted that the Lord is good" (1 Peter 2:2–3).

The author of the letter to the Hebrews chided his readers for their lack of spiritual growth. He said that they should have been eating solid food ("strong meat" in the KJV), but they still needed milk like babies (Hebrews 5:12).

At times, the Word is even compared to honey as when Ezekiel was told, "'Son of man, eat this scroll I am giving you and fill your stomach with it.' So I ate it, and it tasted as sweet as honey in my mouth" (Ezekiel 3:3).

In another well-known metaphor, Paul calls the results of Spirit-filled Christian character the "fruit of the Spirit" (Galatians 5:22).

Sounds like a well-balanced diet.

Think of this book as a buffet as to where you go in. Modern buffets have various stations with different types of food. You can gravitate to the omelet station at brunch. Or the mashed potato and toppings station at a wedding. (A little odd, but tasty.)

Similarly, there is no right or wrong way to approach this book. You don't have to read chapters in numerical or biblically chronological order. However, please read **Chapter 1** first to see Jesus' rationale for studying Him in the Old Testament and to get some working definitions. It's like grabbing your plate at the head of the buffet. Then you can fill that plate any way you choose.

Just an FYI: the section about messianic symbolism in Exodus and the tabernacle, because of its subject matter, is a little heavier reading than some sections. Let's call it the steak section. You won't need a steak knife (or a theological degree), but try to approach it with a clear mind and more than just a few minutes to spare.

Think of this book as a buffet—except that loading up won't hurt you. Forget the saying, "A moment on the lips; a lifetime on the hips." Did you know that the Bible actually praises having a "fat soul"? I've heard it's possible to get sick of sweets if you eat too many. I've never tested this theory because I love sweets and couldn't be neutral. But I know for sure that it's *not* possible to overload on Bible truth. To the contrary, what you'll find never grows stale and becomes sweeter all the time.

So, welcome! I pray that everything you learn will deepen and widen your understanding of Jesus Christ in ways you may not have imagined. And my hope is that at some point in the future when you are in the Old Testament, you will have one of those wonderful *eureka* moments. It will suddenly strike you: "I never noticed that before, but there's Jesus!"

PART I
BEGINNING WITH MOSES

Chapter 1
Last (and Not-So-Last) Words

People tend to put a lot of importance on last words or deathbed statements. Even legal proceedings often lend more weight to them than normal testimony. There have been books written about famous last words from various viewpoints—from the poetic to the profane. The most interesting and pertinent are from those who knew they were dying and wanted to make a final statement.

Last Words
You might expect the last words of writers to be exceptional and many of them are. When poet Emily Dickinson died in 1886, she put it this way, "I must go in, the fog is rising."

O. Henry (William Sidney Porter), the writer of such classic short stories as *The Gift of the Magi*, died in 1910 saying, "Turn up the lights, I don't want to go home in the dark."

Edgar Allan Poe, author of many morbid tales, may have feared going into that dark night. At his death in 1849 he pleaded, "Lord, help my poor soul."

Some have been obsessed with their work or artistry to the point that it became their final voiced thought. When Leonardo da Vinci died in 1519 he said, "I have offended God and mankind because my work did not reach the quality it should have." (We might ask: then whose work did?)

Prolific inventor Thomas Alva Edison, while dying in 1931, was thinking more of another world than the one he'd worked so hard to improve. "It is very beautiful over there," he said as he went to explore it.

However, for the dying statement most connected with his life's work, my vote goes to Dominique Bouhours, a French grammarian whose last words in 1702 were meticulously chosen: "I am about to—or I am going to—die: either expression is correct."

There are always some who live and die, possibly in denial, but in their own little world. "I've never felt better" were the last words of actor Douglas Fairbanks, Sr. in 1939.

No one knows if Broadway extravaganza producer Florenz Ziegfeld was having a vision of coming attractions or was just dreaming, but his last words in 1932 were certainly optimistic: "Curtain! Fast music! Light! Ready for the last finale! Great! The show looks good; the show looks good!"

It should be a surprise to no one that preachers and well-known Christians often die speaking of their faith turning into sight. "Now comes the mystery," evangelist Henry Ward Beecher said.

Famous preacher D. L. Moody tried to describe what he was seeing for those left behind: "Earth recedes. Heaven opens before me. If this is death, it is sweet! There is no valley here. God is calling me, and I must go!"

Writer Joseph Addison wanted his death to be a teachable moment: "See in what peace a Christian can die."

And John Newton, Anglican preacher and author of the hymn "Amazing Grace," affirmed his faith with his dying statement: "I am in the land of the dying, and I am soon going to the land of the living."

Because they were famous men, most of the last words of American presidents were written down for posterity. Father of his country George Washington died in 1799 saying, "I die hard but am not afraid to go."

Not many years later John Quincy Adams passed away (1848) with these words: "This is the last of Earth! I am content."

William McKinley, the twenty-fifth president, was assassinated in 1901. He forgave the man who shot him and said while dying, "Good-bye, good-bye all! It's God's way. His will, not ours, be done."

Although some of these dying words may seem profound, just being in the state of dying doesn't necessarily make last words any more prescient or intelligent. I think particularly of General John Sedgwick, a Union commander who was killed in 1864 during the U.S. Civil War. The last thing he was heard to say was, "They couldn't hit an elephant at this dist . . ."

Not-So-Last Words
While last words are often recorded, there doesn't seem to be much recorded about what people said after they were resurrected. *For obvious reasons!* But didn't you ever wonder how Lazarus answered everything people asked him after Jesus raised him from the dead? (Some have called what happened to the people Jesus raised more *resuscitation* than resurrection because each had to die again.) Maybe Lazarus couldn't remember anything about the four-day period he was dead and entombed, but that wouldn't have stopped anyone from asking. The only thing we're told is that many people came to believe in Jesus because of that miracle (John 11:45).

Think about this: how much more important than talking to Lazarus after he was brought back from the dead would be the ability to talk to Jesus after His own resurrection? Many people did have that privilege. In 1 Corinthians 15:6 Paul wrote that over 500 people saw the resurrected Lord before He ascended back to heaven.

On that first Easter afternoon, Jesus joined two people as they walked on the road to Emmaus (Luke 24:13–35). These two were not part of the 12 hand-picked disciples but part of His larger group of followers. One was named Cleopas. Because women in that day weren't recognized or cited as legally credible sources, some theologians, such as J. I. Packer, have speculated that the deliberately unnamed person might have been Cleopas' wife.

As they walked, Jesus kept them from recognizing Him while asking them what had been happening in Jerusalem. They were shocked anyone didn't know the news: the one many hoped would be their Messiah had been crucified. How did He respond to their grief and dismay?

He said to them, "How foolish you are, and how slow to believe all that the prophets have spoken! Did not the Messiah have to suffer these things and then enter his glory?" And beginning with Moses and all the Prophets, he explained to them what was said in all the Scriptures concerning himself (Luke 24:25–27).

Notice that Jesus didn't pity or baby this grieving pair. Instead He explained to them from their own Scriptures—and the Old Testament was all they had—what had been predicted about the Messiah. He put it quite bluntly that if they had been wise enough (instead of "foolish") and believed what had been written in those Scriptures, they would *not* have been surprised that their Messiah had to suffer. Faith in the promises of the Old Testament could have prevented their distress and grief. Instead, they would have been waiting and anticipating what God would do through the death of His Son.

Graciously, Jesus allowed their ignorance and surprise to become part of a scriptural lesson for all of us on how inadequate our belief system often is—and how a stronger faith could spare us a lot of heartache. This section is the major "proof text," if you need one, for the premise of this book: Jesus Christ appeared throughout the Old Testament.

How do we know? *He said so!*

Wouldn't it have been wonderful if the Holy Spirit had prompted Luke to write down everything Jesus taught them? But we don't have that; we have only what Jesus said to them before He told them all that we'd like to know. Maybe the Lord wanted us to dig it out for ourselves—no *Cliff Notes* on this. We're told that Moses and the prophets wrote about Him. Moses wrote the first five books of the Bible (the Pentateuch). But we also know that there are more references to Christ in the Old Testament than just in the Pentateuch and the prophetic books. In that day saying "Moses and the Prophets" or "the Law and the Prophets" was a way of referring to the whole Old Testament. The expression included, rather than excluded, other historical books and wisdom literature such as Job and the Psalms which also include prophecies and references to Christ.

Whoever the couple Jesus walked with were, for them it became a surprise party in reverse. The One they invited to be their guest of honor entered their home and then surprised them. As they were breaking bread, Jesus allowed them to recognize Him. When they did, He suddenly disappeared from their midst. What did they discuss then? They didn't talk about what He looked like or what His voice sounded like—or even why they hadn't been able to recognize Him at first. They talked about how their hearts burned as He explained the Scriptures to them.

Look Deeply, See Clearly
Do you remember in the 1990s those colorful dot-filled pictures or posters that had a 2D pattern that repeated several times but also had a hidden 3D pattern in the middle? Those pictures split the population into two groups—one group could see the 3D image and one couldn't. I was the latter.

No matter who explained how to do it to me, I could never see the 3D images. My husband and kids saw them. "Oh, look, it's a lion!" "An eagle—fantastic!" "Can't you see that?" No, I couldn't. And I'm still in the frustrated non-seeing group when it comes to those pictures.

The pictures are called autostereograms, and the concept has been around since the 1930s when they were used to study depth perception. The inventor probably never envisioned that his idea would one day be used for books, lunchboxes, and even neckties.

Autostereograms were patented under the name Magic Eye in 1996. You can see a number of them on the Magic Eye website (www.magiceye.com). The website even explains how to see them by making your eyes "diverge":

"Hold the center of the printed image *right up to your nose.* It should be blurry. Focus as though you are looking *through* the image into the distance. *Very slowly* move the image away from your face until the *two squares* above the image turn into *three squares.* If you see four squares, move the image farther away from your face until you see three squares. If you see one or two squares, start over! When you clearly see three squares, hold the page still, and the hidden image will magically appear. Once you perceive the hidden image and depth, you can look around the entire 3D image. The longer you look, the clearer the illusion becomes. The farther away you hold the page, the deeper it becomes. Good Luck!"

Good luck, indeed! Been there, tried that, still can't see it. I looked around the Magic Eye website trying to find a "puzzle" that might be easier than the others. One of them, under the spiritual category, had a beautiful artist's concept of the face of Jesus as its main image. It showed the hidden image below the autostereogram, an image of Jesus as the Good Shepherd with a couple of lambs. Even with that big hint I wasn't able to see it in the picture itself. (Do you think the problem is my computer screen or the computer that is my brain?)

Regardless of my inability to see them, the whole Magic Eye idea seems an apt illustration of the theme of this book. If we consider the whole Bible like a Magic Eye multi-colored, multi-dimensional image, many people are like I've been with the Magic Eye puzzles. They see only the initial picture. They may be impressed with its colors and intricacies, but they haven't learned how to look deeply enough within its pages—especially its Old Testament pages—to see the beautiful hidden picture of Christ. It's not hidden to keep us from seeing, but to be the reward for those willing to look deeper into the things of Scripture. As Deuteronomy 29:29 says, "The secret things belong to the LORD our God, but the things revealed belong to us and to our children forever."

Another point from their instruction is true of looking into the pages of the Bible for images of Christ: "the longer you look, the clearer [He] becomes."

Theo—what?

As we go through many of the books in the Old Testament, we will look at places where Christ appears in a pre-incarnate form—sometimes as a man, sometimes as an angel. Such an appearance has a technical name: a *theophany*, defined as "the appearance of a god in a visible form to a human being." It isn't just a Judeo-Christian term. In the definition "god" has a lower case "g" because in Greek and Roman mythology, and various other religions, their gods were said to appear on earth in human form. (Frequently in mythology those gods were up to no good and sometimes impregnated human women to beget "half-gods.")

There are also many places in the Old Testament where the reference to Christ is personified or viewed symbolically. In those references, we'll see what is called a "type of Christ." The New Testament helps clarify this connection. For example, the Passover lamb is a type of Christ because it was slain for the redemption of the people. Paul made sure we would get this by writing: "Get rid of the old yeast, so that you may be a new unleavened batch—as you really are. For Christ, our Passover lamb, has been sacrificed" (1 Corinthians 5:7).

To make it simpler as we look at references, I will usually call Him "Christ" when He appears in the Old Testament. And I will call Him "Jesus" when the reference is to the New Testament because He was given that human name when He entered the world as a baby.

Prophetically Speaking

There are three kinds of prophecies in the Old Testament. Walt Kaiser, Jr. described them this way in his book, *The Messiah in the Old Testament:*

1. **Direct:** The Old Testament author looked directly at the messianic age, and it is understood to be a prophecy about the Messiah, such as Micah 5:2 where we're told that the Messiah would be born in a village called Bethlehem.
2. **Typical (or "type"):** In this category we have persons, institutions, or events that were divinely designated in the Old Testament text to be models, previews, or pictures of something that was to come in the days of the Messiah. (See J. Sidlow Baxter's definition below.)
3. **Applications:** An example of an application is when the text in the New Testament lets you know how an Old Testament text should or can be applied. For instance Matthew 2:23 says, "and he went and lived in a town called Nazareth. So was fulfilled what was said through the prophets: 'He will be called a Nazarene.'" Here Matthew refers to Isaiah 11:1 where the Messiah is called the "Branch" or *nezer*. Because the Hebrew word sounds like *Nazarene*, it became both an interpretation and possibly a play on words.

One of the clearest definitions of "a type of Christ" is from J. Sidlow Baxter (*Explore the Book*): "God has been pleased to invest certain persons, objects, events, acts, [and] institutions with a pre-figurative meaning, so that besides having a real relationship with their own times they have had a significance reaching far forward into the future."

So with that basic explanation of what we're looking for, let's start looking. We'll begin in Genesis because, as a song about musical notes from *The Sound of Music* says, the beginning is often "a very good place to start."

Chapter 2
The Jesus Moses Knew

I don't often take the time or endure the frustration of arguing with cult members, but many years ago I answered the door and ended up in a discussion with a woman who was a Jehovah's Witness teacher. Trying to shorten the episode, I quickly told her that I was a Christian and didn't believe the way she did. Specifically, I didn't believe that Jesus was a created being or that His brother was Satan.

Launching into her talking points, she declared that we had many beliefs in common—and she didn't think I knew what Jehovah's Witnesses believed. No, I told her, we disagreed on the most basic doctrines because the Bible said Christ is God, part of the Trinity, and that He was not a created being but was, in fact, the Creator.

She seemed flabbergasted when I quoted Colossians 1:15–16: "The Son is the image of the invisible God, the firstborn over all creation. For in him all things were created: things in heaven and on earth, visible and invisible, whether thrones or powers or rulers or authorities; all things have been created through him and for him."

She almost shouted, "That's not in the Bible!"

I got my Bible and showed it to her. Her problem was that it wasn't in *her* Bible—the New World translation that Jehovah's Witnesses use. That verse and many others had been altered in their version to keep members from seeing what their leaders didn't want them to see.

Hebrews 1:2–3 is another reference a cult leader wouldn't want his followers to read because it clearly says [emphasis mine], "... but in these last days he has spoken to us by his Son, whom he appointed heir of all things, and *through whom also he made the universe*. The Son is the radiance of God's glory and the exact representation of his being, sustaining all things by his powerful word. After he had provided purification for sins, he sat down at the right hand of the Majesty in heaven."

These are only a couple of many proof texts that help us see Jesus Christ did not begin in a manger in Bethlehem. He always was.

Beginning with Moses
Eugene Peterson wrote, "More words in our Holy Scriptures are ascribed to Moses than to any other single speaker or writer. The words of Moses, written in the first five books of the Bible, are the foundational words of the revelation of God to us. In the Hebrew tradition, both ancient and modern, everything following the Books of Moses is either commentary or elaboration on Moses. . . . Jesus commonly referred to the Torah ('the Law') simply as 'Moses.' In the early church, Moses is the most prominent ancestral name, whether as leader of the people of God or as mediator of the revelation of God in Torah. Torah and Moses were virtual synonyms in both Judaism and church."

Moses wrote the first book, Genesis, to teach the Jews their history and to show them positive and negative examples of those who followed the Lord. The word *genesis* means "beginning." He wasn't alive at the time anything in Genesis happened, being born near the end of the 300 years of slavery that the Jews experienced in Egypt. He undoubtedly heard the stories passed down through his people by oral tradition. Then God inspired (or "breathed into") him as to what and how to write it.

Genesis is the first book in the five-book series collectively called the *Pentateuch*. This word comes from two Greek words meaning "five" and "useful." The definition fits because they are "five useful books." You may be surprised at just how useful they are as we look at how many places Christ shows up in them.

The Pentateuch is called in Hebrew the *Torah*. We saw in Luke 24 how Jesus walked with two people on the Emmaus road and explained to them His appearances in the Old Testament "beginning with Moses" (Luke 24:27). As the context shows, he was referring to the Torah, the books they knew Moses wrote, not the time period in history in which Moses lived.

However, that was hardly the first time Jesus had referenced His eternal past. Speaking to the Jews, who were supposed to be experts in their own Scriptures, He had said in John 5 verses 39 and 46: "You study the Scriptures diligently because you think that in them you have eternal life. These are the very Scriptures that testify about me.... If you believed Moses, you would believe me, for he wrote about me."

This was one of the many times Jesus challenged the spirituality of the Jewish leaders. By Jesus' day, the leaders of the Jews had added many oral traditions to their God-given Scriptures. They thought their knowledge of the Torah and their very Jewishness were their saving grace. One of their traditional beliefs was that no Jew would ever go to hell. They said that an angel was stationed at the gates of hell to turn back any Jew who might approach and say, "You don't belong here."

Then along came Jesus who not only did miracles they couldn't explain but also deflated their holier-than-thou balloon. He indicted them with the fact that, although they studied the Scriptures, they ignored where those Scriptures pointed. In fact, the word *torah* in Hebrew means "to point in a direction." The Torah *pointed in the direction* of the coming Messiah, Jesus. If they had really believed Moses, they would have believed [in] Jesus.

So let's begin with Moses—"in the beginning"—and follow the path he laid out (the path they should have followed):

The Creator: Genesis 1:1–2
In the very first verse of the Old Testament, we see God the Son in action:

In the beginning God created the heavens and the earth. Now the earth was formless and empty, darkness was over the surface of the deep, and the Spirit of God was hovering over the waters.

The word for "God" in verse 1 is in the plural form, signifying not just God the Father but also God the Son. And verse 2 shows that the Holy Spirit was also involved.

When the Apostle John wrote his first book, he wanted to make sure we understood that Jesus was both eternal and involved in creation. He declared in John 1:1–3:

In the beginning was the Word, and the Word was with God, and the Word was God. He was with God in the beginning. Through him all things were made; without him nothing was made that has been made.

As John Wesley said, "God created the heavens and the earth and didn't even half try." And that Creator-God was Christ.

He Walks with Me: Genesis 3

In the Old Testament we find *theophanies* that are pre-incarnate appearances of Christ. Sometimes at first glance the figure is taken for an angel, but then something happens that proves it is really the Lord. In several places in Genesis, God walks and talks with His children as a person talks with a friend—as He did with Adam and Eve. Genesis 3:8 shows by inference that God had been in the habit of walking and talking with Adam and Eve. But after they sinned by eating the forbidden fruit, they realized things had changed. The next time He came to visit them, they tried to cover their nakedness and hide.

The hymn *In the Garden* (Charles Miles 1912) is about this kind of divine fellowship:

I come to the garden alone
While the dew is still on the roses
And the voice I hear falling on my ear
The Son of God *discloses.*

And He walks with me, and He talks with me,
And He tells me I am His own;
And the joy we share as we tarry there,
None other has ever known.

"None other has ever known" is where the hymn got it a little wrong because many have known that same joy. Christ walked with Enoch (Genesis 5:21–24) and Noah (Genesis 6:9). In Genesis 18 Abraham had three men come to visit him, and we're told plainly that one of them was the Lord.

How can I say that in each of these instances the theophany was the pre-incarnate Christ? In the case of Enoch and Noah, it's an inference derived from the way the persons of the Trinity interact with people throughout the Bible. For instance, we never see the Holy Spirit take a human form. He appeared as a dove at the baptism of Jesus, as a wind and as flames of fire at Pentecost, but never as a human.

I can't think of a time that we see God the Father come to earth in human form. In fact, Jesus said of the Father in John 5:37 that people had "never heard his voice nor seen his form." But we do see Jesus, God the Son in human form, throughout His 33-year ministry on earth recorded in the New Testament. Because Jesus was always the member of the Trinity to interact with people in the New Testament, I can infer that the theophany forms of God in the Old Testament were also the pre-incarnate Jesus.

What's important to remember is that even though Jesus walked with people in a more physical sense in biblical times, He still walks with us today by His presence in our lives through the Holy Spirit. This is what Jesus meant when He said that when He was gone from the earth His followers would do "greater things" than He had done (John 14:12). Have you ever thought about what a remarkable statement that is? Although the works of believers could never be greater in *quality* than the things Jesus did on earth, they can be greater in *quantity* simply because the Holy Spirit can indwell and empower millions of believers at one time all over the world. While He was on earth, Jesus limited Himself in His human body to being in one place at one time.

The Serpent-Crusher: Genesis 3:15

And I will put enmity between you and the woman, and between your offspring and hers; he will crush your head, and you will strike his heel.

Protoevangelium is what this verse is often called. It means "first gospel" and is the first mention of redemption in the Bible. The concept is repeated by Paul in Romans 16:20 as he writes that "the God of peace will soon crush Satan under your feet." Some Bible scholars argue about which Old Testament verses point to Christ, but most agree that this verse clearly does. It was the promise given to Adam and Eve that even though their sin brought them spiritual and physical death, a Redeemer—Christ—would come to undo what the Serpent and their own yearnings had done. The verse was part of a promise that all who believed in Him would be saved on credit until that time came.

Abel, a Type of Christ: Genesis 4:1–2

Eve . . . became pregnant and gave birth to Cain. She said, "With the help of the LORD I have brought forth a man." Later she gave birth to his brother Abel.

The word that Eve used indicated that when she gave birth to her first son, she thought he would be the redeemer. (Thousands of years of history have shown us that our prayers are rarely answered that quickly.) Adam and Eve's son Cain wasn't a redeemer; he was a murderer. Instead, Cain's brother Abel became a type of the redeemer who would come thousands of years later. Abel was a shepherd who listened, obeyed, and brought the kind of sacrifice

God had made known to man that He would accept—a blood sacrifice. There is no evil spoken of Abel. He was hated by his brother and killed without a cause. In each of these aspects, Abel is a type of Christ.

Enoch Walked with God: Genesis 5:21–24
These verses tell us literally that "Enoch walked and continued to walk with God." He began that walk after his son Methuselah was born. Methuselah's name means "when he is gone, it will come." The name shows that, through his relationship with God, Enoch knew some kind of destruction (the Flood) was coming on the earth. But the name also indicates God let Enoch know that the destruction would not come until his son was dead. The fact that Methuselah lived the longest of any human—969 years—shows the patience and grace of God. Enoch became one of two men in the Old Testament who went to heaven without dying. (The other was Elijah.) Hebrews 11:5 says:

By faith Enoch was taken from this life, so that he did not experience death: "He could not be found, because God had taken him away." For before he was taken, he was commended as one who pleased God.

A little girl told the story this way:
Enoch walked and talked every day with God. Each day they walked further and further. They talked about all kinds of things and looked at all the beautiful trees and flowers and animals as they walked. They really enjoyed themselves. Then one day God said, "Enoch, you're closer to My house than yours, why don't you just come home with Me?" So he did.

Where is Christ in this account? The God Enoch walked with—and went home with—was the pre-incarnate Christ.

Chapter 3
A Broken World

Lauren Hillenbrand wrote a best-selling biography on Louis Zamperini, *Unbroken,* which was also made into a movie. Zamperini was a poor boy who grew up to be an Olympic runner in the 1936 Olympics. Later in college he came close to running a four-minute mile. When World War II broke out, he volunteered and served as a B-24 bombardier until his plane went down over the Pacific. He and two others drifted on a raft they made of plane scraps. They survived by catching albatross with their hands and drinking rain water.

After 47 days he and the (by then) one other survivor were picked up by Japanese and taken to a prisoner of war camp. There he was terribly abused but was, as the title indicates, "unbroken" in spirit. However, those two years as a P.O.W. left their mark on him. Returning to the U.S., he struggled with PTSD and alcohol addiction until he heard a message by Billy Graham in 1949 and was saved. Zamperini forgave his captors, including the commander of the camp who had been especially cruel.

Author Lauren Hillenbrand wrote the book in an unusual way. She has an acute form of chronic fatigue syndrome that kept her from traveling to interview her subject in California. (At one point because of her illness, she didn't leave her home for two years.) After Zamperini read an article about Hillenbrand, he sent her his purple heart. In the note that accompanied it he wrote that, because of her suffering, he believed she deserved it more than he did.

What was especially interesting to me as a writer was that Hillenbrand never met Zamperini until after her book about him was published. She wrote it through background research and by having 75 phone conversations with him. (I have written magazine profile pieces on famous people where I wasn't allowed to interview them in person. I did those through phone interviews, and it's not easy.) *Unbroken* was a biography done the hard way.

We call non-fiction books about people's lives biographies if written by others or autobiographies if written by the subjects themselves. American columnist Russell Baker defined the problem: "The biographer's problem is that he never knows enough. The autobiographer's problem is that he knows too much."

Reading the Bible, which includes many partial biographies, we get both aspects. The human writer tells us what he knows (through inspiration) about the people involved in the historical or eyewitness account, but the Holy Spirit gives a deeper aspect. It's like having what we call in novel writing an "omniscient narrator"—one who knows everything that's going on behind the scenes and in the hearts and minds of the characters.

When God writes the story, He is the ultimate *omniscient narrator*.

The Ark and Our Security in Christ: Genesis 6–8

When we come to the time recorded in Genesis 6, the world had become corrupted and mankind so evil that the Lord could only find one righteous man, Noah. Even then it wasn't that Noah was perfect or sinless, for no mere human being is, but that Noah "found grace in the eyes of the LORD" (v. 8 NKJV).

It was an evil world in which life went on as normal with people ignoring God and doing anything they wanted, while having no idea how close they were to destruction. (Interestingly, in Luke 17:26 Jesus said the chaotic "last days" would be "just as it was in the days of Noah.") Noah's life demonstrates that even in the evilest surroundings, it is always possible to walk with God. Pastor Donald Barnhouse said that the lives of Enoch and Noah in that overwhelmingly evil time "show that it is possible to grow a lily in a manure pile."

God obviously talked with Noah, but we're never told that God appeared to him. The story of Noah doesn't involve a theophany. Instead, the ark that God told Noah to build became a beautiful type of Christ. God told Noah exactly how to build the ark, from what materials to use to the dimensions to the placement of the door and window. The ark became the means of (physical) salvation for Noah and his family during the Flood.

Here are some ways the ark is a type of the believer's spiritual and eternal security in Christ:

* The ark had only one door in the side through which Noah's family was told to load the animals and to enter themselves before the rain started. In John 10:9 (ESV) Jesus said, "I am the door." In John 14:6 Jesus reiterated to His disciples that He was the only way.

* There was only one window in the ark and it opened toward heaven. Jesus came to earth to redeem us and was, in a way, a window into heaven. He told His disciples that because they had seen Him, they had seen God (John 14:8–10).

* In Genesis 6:14 the word for the substance Noah was told to use to waterproof the ark is called "pitch." But that same Hebrew word is translated 70 times in the Old Testament: "to make atonement." In Leviticus 17:11 ". . . the blood that makes atonement [serves as pitch] for your soul."

Have you ever noticed what the ark *didn't* have? It had no sails and no rudder or other steering mechanism. The family would be safe, but they had no control over the journey—either its direction or its length.

Genesis 7:14 says that the Lord shut the family in. There was no salvation outside the ark, only judgment and death. But Noah and his family were perfectly secure inside it no matter how much death and destruction was all around them. When we believe in Christ, we are "in Christ." All believers are secure in Christ.

The Semitic Line of Christ: Genesis 9:25–27

Noah showed great faith as he built an ark by faith and saved his family. But after the family was on dry land again, not everything went smoothly. In Genesis 9:20–29 we're disappointed to read that Noah planted a vineyard and used the wine he made to get drunk and pass out naked in his tent. That episode caused his three sons to make a choice as to how they would treat their father in that humiliating condition. Ham dishonored and apparently mocked his father. But in an act of love (that covers a multitude of sins) Shem and Japheth backed into the tent and covered Noah.

When Noah sobered up and found out what happened, he cursed Canaan, which was Ham's line, but blessed the lines of Japheth (most connected with Gentiles or non-Jews) and Shem, through whom the Jews and the Messiah would come. Genesis 9:27 contains a prophecy that God Himself will one day dwell among the Shemites (in the Greek, the "Semites"): "May God extend Japheth's territory; may Japheth live in the tents of Shem, and may Canaan be the slave of Japheth." And as John 1:14 says, the Word—Jesus Christ—did become flesh and make His dwelling (literally "set up His tent") among us, specifically among the Jews.

Noah lived 350 years longer (9:28) and most likely walked with God and served Him faithfully. But this unfortunate incident is recorded—possibly as a warning to us—to watch out lest we fall too. Dr. William Culbertson, for many years president of Moody Bible Institute in Chicago, used to close his public prayers with, "And, Lord, help us to end well." Dr. Culbertson did end well, but not everyone does.

And God Came Down: Genesis 11

Historian Charles Beard wrote, "Whom the gods would destroy, they first make drunk with power." Whereas Noah was drunk on wine, the people that Genesis 11 speaks of were drunk on power. You could say that this was the first United Nations and that their unanimous decision to build a tower to reach heaven was a declaration of war against God.

God had told the people to scatter and repopulate the earth as their population increased after the Flood (9:1). Instead, motivated by fear or pride, they stayed together and built a city and an immense tower for astrological idol worship. They wanted to make a name for themselves, probably hoping others would admire and join them. The main thing missing in their plans was the approval of God.

They made bricks to build an extremely tall ziggurat, which is like a stepped pyramid that can be ascended. At the top was usually a special shrine dedicated to a god or goddess. They weren't actually trying to climb up to heaven to dethrone God. Instead, they apparently hoped that the god or goddess they worshipped would use the staircase to come down from heaven to meet them.

Genesis 11 illustrates perfectly what the Augustinian monk Thomas à Kempis wrote in *On the Imitation of Christ*: "Man proposes, but God disposes." This is a case of be careful what you wish for because God—Christ—did come down. He didn't come to meet them, and it's doubtful He used their stepped pyramid to descend. He came down to inspect and solve the sin problem (11:5–7):

But the LORD came down to see the city and the tower the people were building. The LORD said, "If as one people speaking the same language they have begun to do this, then nothing they plan to do will be impossible for them. Come, let us go down and confuse their language so they will not understand each other."

Warren Wiersbe wrote, "God in heaven is never perplexed or paralyzed by what people do on earth. Babel's conceited 'Let's go up!' was answered by heaven's calm 'Let's go down!'"

Unfortunately, the tower of Babel mentality is still alive and well. Even today many say that if people could just get together and understand each other (sing *Kumbaya*), the world would get better. But God in His foreknowledge knew that the world would *not* be better if everyone got together. That would only escalate the evil people could imagine and do. After all, this was happening within a few hundred years of the time that Genesis 6:5 spoke of in which "every imagination of men's hearts was evil continually." A time when they had a common language and evil became so rampant that God sent a flood that wiped out all humanity except Noah's family.

Christ short-circuited the Babel rebellion by changing the languages of people and geographically scattering them. With a language barrier, they couldn't get together and do much damage (vv. 8–9). The word *babel* sounds like the Hebrew word *balal* which means "confusion." Because of God's judgment, what they had wishfully named their "gate of the gods" became instead their "door to confusion."

And confusion has reigned ever since when mankind tries to build their world without God.

A Broken Man: Job

The Book of Job probably should be placed chronologically about this point in Genesis because it is one of the oldest books. Most commentators believe Job lived in the period around the time of the patriarchs because he acted as high priest for his family, offering sacrifices for them. This would be normal before the Levitical law was given to Moses. After that time, only priests could offer sacrifices.

Hundreds of books have been written and sermons preached about the suffering of Job. No mere human being ever seemed to lose so much so quickly. God accepted a challenge from Satan: to prove that Job, who had been greatly blessed, wasn't just worshipping God because of all that he received. To prove this early in man's history, God allowed Satan to take from Job everything except his life.

One of the problems of suffering is that people think they would be able to face it better if they just knew *why*. Because we rarely find out why, we don't know if that's true. But, if Job had known that he was suffering because God accepted a challenge from Satan, it probably *wouldn't* have made him feel better. It might have made him angry at God. As it was, even though he didn't know *why*, Job never cursed God.

Satan went quickly to work and Job lost all the material belongings that had made him wealthy (Job 1). Far more significant, in one day his ten children died when the house they were meeting in for a celebration collapsed on them. If that was not enough, Job was soon covered from head to foot in boils. The only thing Job had left was his wife, and she encouraged him to curse God and die. Why did Satan take Job's whole family and leave him only his wife? I used to say it was because his wife turned out to be no help to him (2:9). But after living this long, I've come to believe differently. I think that Satan left her there because he knew that as Job saw her suffer— she'd just lost all her children and her wealth too—he would suffer more. And having her lash out at him would make his pain even more excruciating.

So where is Christ in this picture of intense suffering? Out of his pain and confusion (Job 9:33) Job cried out for someone to arbitrate, for someone to be a mediator between him and God. With all that had happened to him, he appealed for representation in some divine court of law. He innately understood that, even though he believed his case was just, as a mortal he couldn't win a dispute with God. What he needed—although he didn't understand it or predict it—was someone both human and divine. Someone who could bridge that divide.

Job referred to this mediator as "my intercessor" and "my friend" (16:19–21). He realized he needed an "advocate with the Father." Millennia later, the apostle John will write that this is exactly what we were given in Christ (1 John 2:1). And Paul will tell Timothy that there is one Mediator, Christ Jesus (1 Timothy 2:5–6).

In one of the most special moments of the Old Testament, Job said that he knows there is such a One living, even in that day:

I know that my redeemer lives, and that in the end he will stand on the earth. And after my skin has been destroyed, yet in my flesh I will see God; I myself will see him with my own eyes—I, and not another. How my heart yearns within me! (Job 19:25–27).

Job hadn't read even one book of Scripture (because there were none written yet), but he knew God. And despite all that had happened, he trusted that God would bring forth the one promised to Adam and Eve in the Garden of Eden (Genesis 3:15). Job called this promised one "my Redeemer." The Hebrew word *goel* used here translates to "kinsman-redeemer." Job declared that this *goel* will one day redeem him. And, even though when that redemption happens Job may have physically died long ago, he knows he will be alive then.

Unlike the New Testament, the Old Testament has so few references to the afterlife, that a whole group of Torah students in Jesus' day—the Sadducees—had declared that there was no resurrection. That this life is all you get. (And I can't resist adding the old humorous line: And that's why they were *SAD, YOU SEE?*) The Book of Job shows us that Job knew better because he knew Christ.

God uses pain to bring us to the place of submission. In *The Problem of Pain* C. S. Lewis wrote, "God whispers to us in our pleasures, speaks in our conscience, but shouts in our pains: it is His megaphone to rouse a deaf world."

We don't see Christ appear to Job. But at the end of the book, God and Job have a conversation where God does most of the talking, explaining how a finite man like Job can't expect to understand the mind of God. Job realizes that, although he was "upright," he wasn't perfect. He begins to see himself as God sees him. He humbles himself and confesses that he had been talking about things he didn't understand. He realizes that anything God does is right and must be accepted by faith (42:1–6).

Job had wanted to know *why*. At the end of the book, he still doesn't know the *why* behind his suffering. But he meets the *Who* and finds that is enough.

Chapter 4
Abraham's Day

I was about 40 pages into reading a novel when I realized that a lot wasn't being mentioned, and it was hard to understand all that what was going on. Maybe I had missed something.

I went to the page in front that contained the author's previous books. There was a list and a small author's note that said, "Although most of these books are stand-alone, several should be read in order." Sure enough, the book I was reading was the second—a sequel instead of volume one. After I got the first book at the library and read it, I returned to the sequel and everything became clear.

The Bible is a little like that. If you were only to read the New Testament and had no knowledge of the Old Testament, you would learn a lot but you wouldn't have the knowledge you need to see the total picture. God's interaction with people didn't begin in New Testament days but thousands of years before. When you read the New Testament, you are reading the sequel.

There are places where Jesus, as He walked on earth, talked about His eternality or His interactions with people in Old Testament days, sometimes specifically speaking of one individual. For instance, in John 8:56 as Jesus spoke to the Jews He said: "Your father Abraham rejoiced at the thought of seeing my day; he saw it and was glad."

Because Abraham wasn't one of the two Old Testament saints who appeared with Jesus on the Mount of Transfiguration (Moses and Elijah in Matthew 17:1–8), we assume that Abraham must have seen the "day" of Christ in his own lifetime. Many believe that when God told Abraham to offer his son Isaac as a sacrifice, recorded in Genesis 22, Abraham "saw" that day.

Abraham and His Seed: Genesis 12

When we come to chapter 12 we find a new beginning—in the book of beginnings—in the covenant God gives Abraham. Previously the narrative had been about many people, but suddenly it narrows and God puts the spotlight on one man and his family. The final three quarters of Genesis tell the story of Abraham and the first three generations of his line. Abraham is also mentioned 74 times in the New Testament. In Acts 7:2–3 Stephen began preaching just before he was martyred:

"Brothers and fathers, listen to me! The God of glory appeared to our father Abraham while he was still in Mesopotamia, before he lived in Harran. 'Leave your country and your people,' God said, 'and go to the land I will show you.'"

God appeared to Abraham (at that time his name was Abram, but we'll call him Abraham here for clarity). We aren't told how God originally appeared to Abraham, but these would have been theophanies in which Christ was the person of God who met with Abraham. Although there could have been more, Genesis records seven communications between God and Abraham.

In the first appearance, God called Abraham from his home in Ur of Chaldees. He was to leave a city that archaeology tells us was so advanced that it even had indoor plumbing and he was to live in tents in a barbaric land. And Abraham, who by all indications had been an idol worshipper, obeyed even though he had no idea of his destination. As someone said, he went out "going, not knowing."

The Bible says that God talked with Abraham as a man talks with his friend. Abraham wasn't called because of any inherent goodness in himself but because, like Noah, he found unmerited grace in the eyes of the Lord.

In Genesis 12:2–3 we see that God pronounced a curse or blessing on people and nations depending on how Abraham and his descendants were treated. The curse placed on nations who have persecuted Jews is evident in the pages of history. All of them have been destroyed or reduced to a minor world player. Where are the Hittites or the Canaanites now? The Greeks desecrated the Jewish temple under Antiochus Epiphanes and then lost power to Rome. Greece never regained world power. In 70 A.D. Rome destroyed Jerusalem. It took several more centuries, but the mighty Roman Empire did fall. Spain was reduced to fifth-rate nation status after the Inquisition in which they persecuted the Jews. Even Britain lost her world empire after she broke faith with Israel in more modern times.

The covenant that God gave Abraham included wonderful promises. He promised to show him a land, to make him into a great nation, and to use that nation to bless the whole world. The missionary mandate of the church can be said to have started with Abraham, before there was a church. We are *blessed* so that we might become a *blessing.*

The blessing that God promised Abraham has been fulfilled in part. That blessing is Christ. In Philippians 3:4–9 Paul wrote that, as a natural-born Jew, the blessings and the promises were his. But as a Messianic Jew, he knew that those promises could only be completed through Jesus Christ. We each have spiritual redemption through Christ when we believe in Him and accept His death for us, but one day the whole world will be physically redeemed at His Second Coming.

Melchizedek, a Type of Christ: Genesis 14
Even though Abraham was a peaceful man, he became involved in a war. There were five city-states in the plain of Jordan that had been put into subjection by a confederation of the kings of four eastern city-states. The five finally had enough of being ruled over by the four and revolted. Naturally, the four eastern kings weren't going to take the revolt lying down, so a war ensued. The four kings with their armies invaded the plain of Jordan. If there had been newspapers in that day, the headline *WAR!* would have covered everything above the fold.

The armies of the four kings were apparently better fighters than those of the five kings. The four kings won and even pushed their adversaries into slime pits (v. 10) before they fled for their lives and higher ground. The victorious kings took material spoils of war plus area residents as slaves. And Lot, who had first looked at Sodom and eventually moved into Sodom, was taken prisoner with his family.

Abraham stayed out of the conflict until he heard that Lot had been captured. Out of love for his relatives, he armed his 318 servants, chased the invaders for 100 miles, freed the prisoners, and recovered everything the armies had taken. Those untrained servant soldiers had a secret weapon—they had God on their side.

After Abraham's victory, in one of the most symbolic stories in Genesis, we meet Melchizedek. He is the King of Salem but is also described as priest of *El Elyon*, God Most High. When Melchizedek brings bread and wine to refresh Abraham, he becomes a type of Christ, the One who instituted the Lord's Supper which involves bread and wine. He blesses Abraham in verse 19 and Abraham then gives Melchizedek a tithe (a tenth) of the material spoils of war. The enslaved people are all set free.

Hebrews 7:1–3 says that Melchizedek is King of Righteousness and King of Peace and is "without father or mother . . . ." However, that doesn't mean he was supernatural and had no parents, as some have thought. It means that, unlike later priests who would be required to come through the Levitical line of Aaron, the tribal lineage of this first priest would make no difference. Melchizedek as both king and priest becomes a perfect type of Christ who is King of kings and eternal High Priest. (Jesus also wasn't from the tribe of Levi but from the tribe of Judah.) In the Mosaic order to come, the offices of kings and priests would be legally separated. But this *prequel* version hints at the One who will fulfill those roles in the New Testament.

The Lord Who Sees Me: Genesis 16:7–13

Every time I read this section, I think of television soap operas. Maybe that's because the story line seems a little like a soap opera. After Sarah insists Abraham sleep with Hagar—in order to have a child she could rear as her own—Hagar becomes pregnant. Then Hagar becomes proud of her new role and comes to despise Sarah. So Sarah mistreats Hagar. Then Hagar runs away. (See what I mean.)

The "angel of the Lord" comes to her in the desert by a spring or well. But this is no ordinary angel. We know it is the pre-incarnate Christ because of what He says in verses 10 to 13 [emphasis mine]:

The angel added, "I will increase your descendants so much that they will be too numerous to count." The angel of the LORD also said to her: "You are now pregnant and you will give birth to a son. You shall name him Ishmael, for the LORD has heard of your misery. He will be a wild donkey of a man; his hand will be against everyone and everyone's hand against him, and he will live in hostility toward all his brothers."

Doesn't this beautifully show the grace of God? Christ made one of his theophany appearances to an Egyptian slave girl who was probably not a believer and who had become pregnant by Abraham (a believer) through no fault of her own. He tells Hagar to go back and submit to Sarah and to name the child Ishmael, which means "God shall hear."

Hagar needed a name for the One who had spoken to her, so she called Him *El Roi*. "You are the God who sees me," she said, "I have now seen the One who sees me." He is the God who saw Hagar and the God who sees each of us. That is a wonderful thought, but I especially like an alternate way of translating it: "Did I ever look at anything else after He gazed upon me?"

Verses 11 to 12 seem especially prophetic as Christ described the kind of son she will have. Ishmael's line became the Arabic nations, and his descendants today are mostly followers of Islam. As the world deals with terrorism caused by radical Islamic hatred toward non-Muslims ("the infidel"), many of Ishmael's descendants have fulfilled this prophecy. They have continued to live in hostility toward their brothers (the Jews) and the world around them.

After Christ spoke with her, Hagar obeyed and returned to Abraham's camp. The fact that Abraham named the baby *Ishmael* shows that Hagar told him about God visiting her. And Abraham believed that she too had been spoken to by God.

The Lord Visits Abraham: Genesis 17:1–5
When Abram was ninety-nine years old, the LORD *appeared to him and said, "I am God Almighty; walk before me faithfully and be blameless. Then I will make my covenant between me and you and will greatly increase your numbers." Abram fell facedown, and God said to him, "As for me, this is my covenant with you: You will be the father of many nations. No longer will you be called Abram; your name will be Abraham, for I have made you a father of many nations.*

After the promise of a coming child was originally given to Abraham and Sarah (when Abraham was 75), they had waited ten years with no pregnancy. Apparently that's all Sarah could stand. She had talked Abraham into sleeping with Hagar, the events of chapter 16 happened and, in the eleventh year since the promise was given, Hagar gave birth to Ishmael. Abraham was 86. As chapter 17 begins, Ishmael is 13 and Abraham is 99.

The Lord appears to Abraham again, and Abraham falls on his face. Christ reveals Himself as *El Shaddai*, God Almighty, the All-Powerful One. At this point He changes Abram's name (*exalted father*) to Abraham (*father of a multitude*) to emphasize the importance of God's purpose and promise which will be realized through Abraham's line of descendants. This is the first time this name of God is used; it's not one that Abraham has known before.

The Hebrew name "*El Shaddai*" (shuh-DYE) is translated as "Almighty" 48 times in the Old Testament (31 of them in Job) and in the New Testament about 10 times. It's almost always translated "Almighty." "*El*" is the name of God that speaks of power; but there isn't total agreement on what *Shaddai* means. Some say it means "to be strong"; others say it means "mountain" or "breast" with the idea of a strength that can comfort and sustain. Combining those, *El Shaddai* can mean "the all-powerful and all-sufficient God who can do anything and meet any need."

I first became familiar with the name *El Shaddai* in 1982 when a young woman named Amy Grant recorded a song by the same name. I bought her album *Age to Age* and played it over and over. The song was written by John Thompson and a young man named Michael Card, a seminary graduate whose lyrics go deep. In 1983 *El Shaddai* won the Dove Award Song of the Year and Michael Card won Songwriter of the Year. The lyrics include several Hebrew names of God and tell part of the story of Abraham as the song says that through God's love and through a ram He "saved the son of Abraham." (Because of copyright laws I can't put the song here, but you can find it easily on the internet.)

The Lord, the pre-incarnate Christ, visited Abraham and Sarah to tell them that the child who was promised—the one through whom the line of the Messiah would come—would be born the next year. Notice what verses 1 to 2 say: "the LORD appeared to him and said, 'I am God Almighty; walk before me faithfully and be blameless. Then I will make my covenant between me and you and will greatly increase your numbers.'"

As Christ assures Abraham that the promise of a son is about to come true, He says "I will" about 12 times, reaffirming the covenant that He first made in Genesis 12. Also in this chapter, the Lord institutes the sign of the covenant which is circumcision.

The Lord is about to do the miraculous. It is important that Abraham know Christ as *El Shaddai* because the God who can do anything is the one who can open Sarah's dead womb and produce a miraculous birth. As in the birth of Jesus to Mary, the actual miracle will be enacted in and through the woman.

It's interesting to note that Abraham was not sterile. He had fathered Ishmael and even though he was younger then, Genesis 25 will prove that he can still father children naturally. (He remarries after Sarah's death and they have six sons.) The inability to have children had apparently been Sarah's physical problem in her youth, and she is past the age of it ever being possible.

Someone put it this way: "Sarah's womb was a tomb." But, He is the God of Resurrection. As the Lord asks Abraham (18:14), "Is anything too hard for the Lord?" (Note how similar this is to what the angel Gabriel will say to the Virgin Mary: *"For nothing is impossible with God"* Luke 1:37.)

After 25 years, the long-awaited son is about to be born to Sarah and Abraham. And through their line will come the long-awaited Son who will give His life to save mankind.

Chapter 5
The Jesus Abraham Knew

Can you remember a time you became so aggravated at someone close to you that either you or the other person "weren't speaking"? I heard about a couple of spinster sisters who had an argument. Because they couldn't afford to live apart, they drew a line down the middle of their home. Each sister stayed on her own side of it for over 30 years, not speaking to the other sister until one of them died. At the end, when asked, the surviving sister couldn't remember exactly what the original argument had been about.

In Genesis 17 we saw the pre-incarnate Christ appear to Abraham for the fifth time as a theophany. What we might *not* have noticed is that as chapter 17 began, it is the first recorded time that God has spoken with Abraham in 13 years since he and Sarah acted on their plan to have a child thru Hagar. In a practical interpretation, we might see that as Abraham being "out of fellowship" with God for 13 years.

Abraham had been used to talking with God frequently, building altars to Him, and worshipping Him. He was also used to having God talk with him and occasionally appear to him as He does in chapter 17 and 18. But there is no mention of an altar or an appearance during those 13 silent years. Abraham may have been going through the same worship practices as he had done before, but something was different. There was a break in the fellowship because Abraham and Sarah had done it their way. They tried to fulfill God's promise to them because they thought He wasn't acting quickly enough. And, they got the same result we get when we try to help God out rather than wait on His timing: a break in fellowship.

We don't know if Abraham realized that there was a problem and confessed his and Sarah's sin, but man's unfaithfulness can't negate the faithfulness of God. As 1 Timothy 2:13 says, "if we are faithless, he will remain faithful, for he cannot disown himself." The conversation begins again. God shows up and reiterates His promise that this couple will have their own biological child.

In chapter 17 He assured Abraham of it but didn't give a time. In chapter 18 He tells him that it will happen the next year. At this time Abraham was 99 and Sarah was 89. They greeted this promise with laughter but also some skepticism. God knows our hearts and He knew exactly how much joy was in their laughter and how much doubt. Because of their ages not changing, Genesis 18 apparently takes place sometime in the same year as Genesis 17, possibly even a few days or weeks later.

The Lord Who Came to Dinner: Genesis 18
One day Abraham sees three strangers coming toward his encampment. He didn't know them, but that didn't matter. The first law of the Middle East was that you had to be hospitable to strangers. Abraham rushed to invite them in and began having a wonderful meal prepared for them. Some of it he even fixed himself. He told Sarah about the visitors, but a woman didn't help entertain men visitors so she stayed out of sight baking bread as he asked. (Three *seahs* or measures of flour equal about five gallons. She was going to make sure they were well fed and had large doggie bags.)

The men ask about his wife and call her "Sarah" which was the new name God had given her only shortly before (17:15), a name not known by others. In verse 10 the Lord tells Abraham "I will return" and that Sarah will have a son the next year. He reaffirms the long-standing promise but sets a time. And He shows that He knows what Sarah is thinking hidden away in a tent as she laughs at that promise. Answering her doubt, the Lord reassures Abraham that nothing is too hard for Him.

Abraham soon realizes that he is speaking with God—the pre-incarnate Christ—and two angels. Christ shares with Abraham (because he is His friend) what He plans to do about Sodom, and the two angels go off toward that city. Verses 17–19 is like a soliloquy in a play in which we're allowed to see that God was thinking about how much He should tell Abraham. God doesn't tell us everything, but He often tells us some of His plans to help us trust Him more. That may be why He gives us a lot of information about the Second Coming even though we may not be living in the time it is fulfilled. Jesus said He has called His followers His friends and He described that time coming as similar to "the days of Lot" (Luke 17:28–30) in which "people were eating and drinking, buying and selling, planting and building. But the day Lot left Sodom, fire and sulfur rained down from heaven and destroyed them all."

The people of Sodom had ignored God and their culture had become so degraded that God came down to destroy them as a lesson to others. God tells Abraham that He has heard a great outcry. That outcry would have come from those being harmed by the rampant sexual perversion of Sodom and Gomorrah. In places with rampant sexual perversion, there are always many victims.

After the angels left, verse 22 says that "Abraham remained standing before the Lord." But David Roper writes in *Seeing God*: "The traditional Hebrew text states just the opposite. The original version tells us that God was actually standing before Abraham, patiently waiting for him to speak. As written, the text underscores God's passion to communicate with all of us. He, as in Abraham's day, stands continually before us, drawing us out, listening to our hearts, waiting to reveal His own."

Abraham's Request: Genesis 18

Abraham takes this opportunity to bring up what has been heavy on his heart: the safety of his nephew Lot and his family. It says in James 4:8 that Abraham drew near to the Lord. The Hebrew word means "to come to court to argue a case." He wasn't just being argumentative, but he did try to make a case before the Lord—a case based on the Lord's justice (v. 25). "Will not the Judge of all the earth do right?" Abraham asks.

He went about it from a logical/human wisdom viewpoint, declaring that surely—with the power to stop it—God would not destroy believers with unbelievers. (Yet Jesus will declare in Luke 13:4, as in the instance of the tower in Siloam falling, that bad things *do* happen to believer and nonbeliever alike.)

At this point Abraham becomes an intercessor and an advocate for any godly people who might be in Sodom. He hopes Lot's family members are among them, but he may not be sure of that either. We wouldn't guess that Lot was a believer if the New Testament hadn't told us that he was "a righteous man who was greatly distressed by the sensual conduct of the wicked." He was distressed by the things that went on in Sodom (2 Peter 2:6–9) but *not distressed enough* to move away or become an effective culture warrior against it. The extent of what he did may have been to complain to those who would listen: "What is the world coming to?"

Abraham was a real man of prayer. Lloyd Ogilvie has said, "Prayer is God's idea. Our desire to pray is the result of [H]is greater desire to talk with us. He has something to say when we feel the urge to pray."

On this side of the Cross, we have developed an almost formulaic style of prayer based on what we learn in the New Testament: that we are to pray to the Father, in the name and will of the Son, and that we will be guided and enabled in our praying by the Holy Spirit. But in the Old Testament there were no such defined guidelines. Patriarchs spoke with God without depending on any formula. Here Abraham doesn't close his eyes and kneel down; he speaks with the pre-incarnate Christ face to face as he intercedes for others.

Christ stands before Abraham and hears him out as he goes through a countdown of "but if there are . . . [this many], would you still destroy Sodom?" entreaties. Sometimes Abraham is criticized for stopping at ten people in his prayer. Maybe he got down to that and said to himself, "there has to be a stopping point; there has to be a penalty for such blatant sin." Maybe he felt he was being repetitious and "bothering God." Or maybe he, like us at times, was praying around the subject instead of asking outright for his real request: "Lord, please save Lot and his family and do whatever You want with the rest of them."

Someone has said, "Never are we more like Christ than when we are interceding." To be an effective pray-er, we must understand the power of God and we must empathize with the needs of those for whom we pray.

In Chuck Swindoll's book, *Abraham,* he said that the first prayer he ever heard was his mother's and had just nine words: "God help you if you ever do that again!"

He went on to write more seriously about prayer and to say that of all the people he knows who are great pray-ers, none have a hard heart. If you really pray for others, you can't have a hard heart. Abraham didn't have a hard heart. As much trouble as his nephew Lot had caused him and as selfish as he'd shown himself to be, Abraham didn't disown him. Think about how ungrateful Lot was—moving back into Sodom after Abraham saved him from captivity (Genesis 14). The natural thing would have been for Abraham to cut off all contact with his undeserving nephew Lot and let him go his way. But Abraham still loved him and his family and prayed for them.

When I think of prayer requests, I often think of what was written by an anonymous Confederate soldier:

I asked God for strength that I might achieve.
I was made weak that I might learn humbly to obey.
I asked God for health that I might do greater things.
I was given infirmity that I might do better things.
I asked for riches that I might be happy.
I was given poverty that I might be wise.

I asked for power that I might have the praise of men.
I was given weakness that I might feel the need of God.
I asked for all things that I might enjoy life.
I was given life that I might enjoy all things.

I got nothing I asked for
But everything I had hoped for . . .
Almost despite myself my unspoken prayers were answered.
I'm among all men most richly blessed.

Abraham will not get exactly what he prayed for, but he'll get the essence of what he was asking for. Notice the grace and mercy of Christ: IF even ten believers could be found, He would spare the city. As it happens, there won't be ten and He'll destroy the city, but He'll bring out the ones Abraham is praying for anyway. This is what Paul said about the merciful nature of God: that "He does exceedingly abundantly more than we could ask or think" (Ephesians 3:20).

A Promise Is a Promise
Has anyone ever promised you something that meant a lot to you and then broke that promise?

When I was five, my father promised that he would get me a horse someday. Four years later, my family was transferred to an Air Force base in New Mexico. There I took horse-back riding lessons and spent a lot of time at the local stables. It became obvious to me that the time was right for me to receive my horse. Finally, I asked my father when he was going to buy my horse. Imagine my shock when he said he'd never promised me any such thing! (A cautionary tale for parents not to promise little children something thinking they'll forget about it. They don't!)

We may need to remind ourselves occasionally that the promises God makes to us are unbreakable. As with Abraham, some of God's promises aren't immediate; we're asked to wait. For instance, we're promised a new body that will (in heaven) be redeemed from this old world of sin and pain. But, if you're reading this, you're a person-in-waiting for that promise, as I am who write this. However, there will never be a time when God goes back on His word. "A promise is a promise" is nowhere truer than when applied to the promises of God. Our present and eternal security depends on His faithfulness.

Abraham's Promised son and God's Promised Son
It might be helpful before we begin looking at texts to look at some points of comparison between Isaac and Jesus Christ:

1. Both had been promised before they came.
2. The announcement of each birth seemed incredible to those hearing it.
3. There was a long period between the initial promise and its fulfillment: for Isaac 25 years and for Jesus, through Abraham's line, about 2,000 years.
4. Both births came in God's perfect timing. For Jesus, Galatians 4:4 says it was in "the fullness of time."
5. They were both miraculous births. Sarah had passed the time of being able to have a child. Jesus had no earthly father; He was born to a virgin.
6. Isaac and Jesus were each the joy and delight of their fathers.
7. Both sons were obedient to their father, even unto death.

A Type of Christ's Sacrifice: Genesis 22
Some say that this chapter is one of the ten greatest in the Bible. This is the seventh appearing of Christ to Abraham. Here the Lord asks him to do what would seem impossible for a loving father whose hope for the promised line of descendants was tied up in Isaac living and having children. Hebrews 11:17-19 explains it a little:

By faith Abraham, when God tested him, offered Isaac as a sacrifice. He who had embraced the promises was about to sacrifice his one and only son, even though God had said to him, "It is through Isaac that your offspring will be reckoned." Abraham reasoned that God could even raise the dead, and so in a manner of speaking he did receive Isaac back from death.

Why was Abraham willing to obey this horrific request? The New Testament reveals what the Old Testament leaves veiled. Abraham trusted God. He believed if he had to go through with the sacrifice—kill Isaac and burn his body—that God would raise him up again. Think about it: this was *before* there had ever been anyone raised from the dead.

It is a story of great faith on Abraham's part. But it is also a story of the faith of Isaac who was not a child (unlike in children's Bible storybook pictures), but a young man at this time. The Hebrew word used for Isaac in verse 6 is the same as the word used elsewhere for an "armed soldier." And an old Hebrew exposition of the passage says, "he laid the wood upon him in the form of a cross." To carry a load of wood up a mountain would not be something expected of a young child.

Some wonder how Abraham could have even considered sacrificing his son, let alone to take the journey up Mount Moriah and be ready to plunge the knife into him when God stopped him. God was testing Abraham's faith, but Abraham didn't know it was a test.

This was nothing like those cases in the news of mothers hearing what they believe is the voice of God telling them to kill their children, and they drive their car into the river to drown them. What those women heard came from deep-seated psychosis (or possibly voices from demonic realms). But Abraham had talked with God many times. He was familiar with the Lord's voice and knew better than to mistake it. Also, remember that child sacrifice was common in Abraham's day in the cultures around him. And the Pentateuch hadn't been written yet forbidding the practice. Even though Abraham had never imagined such a command coming from the God he knew, the text shows us that He was willing to obey even though he didn't understand. He didn't delay. When the command came, he got up early the next morning and started the trip.

Although it's doubtful God would ever ask anything equally difficult of us, we can learn from Abraham's response. Amy Carmichael, a missionary who spent most of her life ministering to children she saved from temple prostitution in India, wrote a friend who was going through a painful experience, "I will say what our Heavenly Father said to me long ago, and says to me still very often: 'See in it a chance to die.'" No wonder that when Elisabeth Elliot wrote a biography of Amy Carmichael, she called it *A Chance to Die*.

That kind of dying is the kind Jesus talked about: dying to self, taking up your cross and following Him. In this test, Abraham had the chance to die. By putting Isaac on the altar, he was laying it all on the altar: his natural love for his late-in-life son, his marriage (what would Sarah say if he killed their son?) and his hopes and dreams for his future posterity. He did literally what Jesus would talk about thousands of years later—he put God above his family, seeming to hate them in comparison to the love he had for God.

Joe Bayly, who was president of David C. Cook publishing (a Christian publisher I used to work for), lost three of his seven children to death—one 18 days after surgery, another at five years old from leukemia, and a third at 18 years old from a sledding accident plus hemophilia. He may have begun to feel as Abraham must have felt when he was asked to sacrifice his son. Without a great faith, it could seem to be more than anyone should be asked to endure. Joe became so familiar with death invading his life that he wrote a great book on it called, *The View from the Hearse.* Publishers later balked at the title and retitled it *The Last Thing We Talk About*. After his teenage boy died, he wrote "A Psalm on the Death of an 18-Year-old Son" (*Psalms of My Life*, Tyndale, 1978). It began:

*What waste Lord
this ointment precious
here outpoured
is treasure great
beyond my mind to think.
For years
until this midnight
it was safe
contained
awaiting careful use
now broken
wasted
lost.
The world is poor
so poor it needs each drop
Of such a store...*

But by the end of the lengthy poem, Joe Bayly has arrived where Abraham was—not understanding but still relinquishing what he cherished:

*O spare me Lord forgive
that I may see
beyond this world
beyond myself
Your sovereign plan
or seeing not
may trust You
Spoiler of my treasure.
Have mercy Lord
here is my quitclaim.*

Abraham dug deep into his faith to give God his "quitclaim" to the life of Isaac. Genesis 22 gives us a beautiful picture of the sacrifice of Christ at Calvary as Abraham and Isaac "went together" to the top of the ridge of Mount Moriah (the same ridge on which Jerusalem sits, where the temple was built, and where Jesus would be crucified). Isaac becomes a type of Christ as he submits to his father's will and is willing to die. Abraham is a type of God the Father who offers his son up as a sacrifice. The difference is that Abraham and Isaac did not understand the *why* involved in what was happening. At Calvary, God the Father and Christ the Son "went together" knowing exactly what was necessary and that it was the only way to redeem mankind from the eternal penalty of sin.

God spared Abraham what He did not spare Himself (Romans 8:32). God stopped Abraham from sacrificing Isaac, but He would not stop those who crucified Jesus. In John 10:17–18 Christ spoke not of being "killed" but willingly laying His life down.

Likewise, Isaac could have easily kept himself from being put on the altar by his over 100-year-old father, but he chose to submit. Jesus, despite the agony of His prayer time in the garden of Gethsemane in which He asked if this cup could pass from Him, submitted entirely to the Father's will. Abraham was prophetic when he told Isaac that God would provide—Himself—a lamb for the sacrifice. There was a ram caught in the bushes, a substitute supplied for Isaac. But for Christ, the "Lamb of God who takes away the sin of the world" (John 1:29), there was no substitute. He had to die as the only suitable—perfect and sinless—sacrifice for sin. And the substitute for you and me.

Chapter 6
Isaac, the Quiet Man

Those who've heard Chuck Swindoll preach know that he often uses humor in his messages. Some who listened to him on the radio have written him letters that read like this, "Don't ever stop laughing, Chuck. Yours is the only laughter that comes into our home." After he spoke at a conference, Chuck mentioned receiving a somewhat happier letter from a woman:

Dear Chuck,
Humor has done a lot to help me in my spiritual life. How could I have raised 12 children, starting at age 32, and not have a sense of humor? After your talk last night, I was having fellowship with friends I met here. I told them I got married at age 31. I didn't worry about getting married. I did leave my future to God's will. But every night I hung a pair of men's pants on the bed and knelt down and prayed this prayer: "Father in heaven, hear my prayer. And grant it if You can. I've hung a pair of trousers here. Please fill them with a man."

The lady with 12 children certainly had her prayer answered as she got married and raised quite a family.

Isaac, the Bridegroom: Genesis 24
As we come to Genesis 24, we see a long chapter that begins with a father's desire to see his son married. It's about a marriage proposal by proxy and possibly the first instance of a mail-order bride. After Abraham receives his son back, as if from the dead, he still has an impediment to becoming the "father of multitudes" which is the meaning of his new name. Isaac is 40 years old. He's single with no girlfriend in sight. This can't stand. In the normal Middle Eastern

way of things—and much of the world for most of history—the father decides to arrange a marriage for his son.

Abraham is 140 at this time (Genesis 21:5; 25:20) and is looking forward to those grandkids. But he knows enough about the people who live around him (Canaanites) to know what kind of daughter-in-law he *doesn't* want birthing them. He also doesn't want to send his son on a long journey. This is the son of promise; Abraham wants to keep him close and safe.

The man Abraham decides to send is unnamed. Let's just call him "the servant." Abraham trusted him with this most important task, so important that he made him swear not to get a wife for Isaac from among the Canaanite women (a line that was cursed and would eventually be driven out of the land) but instead from Abraham's relatives. He is to go back to his homeland to get a bride for his son. *Twice* he tells the servant not to take his son from his side again, even if the woman refuses to come with him.

A camel caravan could average about 25 miles per day. At this pace, the servant's ten-camel, 900-mile roundtrip would have taken less than a month and a half. Abraham sends the servant with specific instructions and no doubt with prayer. But the servant is also a man of faith. He prays for guidance to find the right girl (vv. 12-14) and for there to be a specific way of recognizing her, which he details for the Lord. (Note: This isn't the best way to pray as God has different ways of leading us and we shouldn't presume to tell Him which is best.)

When the servant reaches his destination, he comes to a well which was a natural gathering place for women. He is still praying about his search but before he is finished, he sees a beautiful young woman named Rebekah (vv. 15-16). She turns out to be Isaac's cousin of some second or more degree or "removed" level (v. 48 says she is the granddaughter of Abraham's brother).

Rebekah not only gives the servant a drink of water but also volunteers to water his camels. How much can ten camels drink? About 40 gallons each = 400 gallons. It might take 100 trips from the well to the trough in at least a two-hour period. While she is doing this, she is unknowingly demonstrating that she is humble, kind, helpful, and hard-working. God has graciously answered the servant's prayer exactly as he asked. He gives her gold jewelry and asks to be taken to her home where he can stay overnight with her family. She obliges in that too.

This is the longest chapter in Genesis, partly because the reader is given the details and then the servant repeats everything that has happened to Rebekah's family. The servant tells her about the wealth of Isaac's father and that Isaac is the heir. His bride will have all that he has. As added proof, he gives the family valuable gifts (he came with ten camels loaded with stuff). The value more than covers the dowry or bride price. He might have said Isaac was a wonderful person, smart and good-looking, but the main purpose in an arranged marriage was for the bride to have economic security. He proves Rebekah will have it. Although the family wants her to stay with them ten more days, the servant says they need to get back. Is Rebekah willing to go with him the next day? She says, "I will go" (v. 58).

It might seem odd that the Lord uses so much descriptive space for the story of an arranged marriage. But maybe it's also the longest chapter in Genesis to draw our attention to the fact that there is more to it than the literal story of a beautiful young woman named Rebekah who accepts the proposal of a young man sight unseen and rides off to marry him. The chapter is chock full of types, pictures, and previews—not only of Christ but of each person of the Godhead and the Church.

More than One Type

Remember J. Sidlow Baxter's definition of a *type* from Chapter 1: "God has been pleased to invest certain persons, objects, events, acts, [and] institutions with a pre-figurative meaning, so that besides having a real relationship with their own times they have had a significance reaching far forward into the future."

This chapter contains at least four *types*, given here in the order of their appearance:

Abraham is a type of God the Father who, after receiving His Son back from the dead, sends the Holy Spirit (often seen in a serving/helping role) to earth to bring back a bride for the Son. The bride is the Father's love gift to the Son, as well as the way by which human progeny will be brought into His family. Notice that this marriage does not—even in the type—begin with the love of the couple for each other, but with the *choice* of the Father to call a bride for His Son. This speaks of a number of things which involve weighty theological subjects, such as calling, election, and predestination. But overall it speaks of the sovereignty of God. He chooses; He decides.

The servant, a type of the Holy Spirit, in Genesis 24 goes to the far country and testifies to the prospective bride and her family about the father, the riches of his house, and the son who is waiting to receive her (John 15:26; 16:13–14). He then protects and escorts the bride to her new home. We can imagine that the servant, who had told Rebekah some things about Isaac to convince her to come, would tell her a lot more about him as they traveled. Similarly, the Holy Spirit lets us know enough about Christ to accept Him, but He continues through our earthly journey to teach us more and more about Christ (John 14:26). When the Holy Spirit leaves the earth at the Rapture, He takes the Church, the Bride of Christ, to meet Christ in the air.

Rebekah is a type of the Bride of Christ, which is comprised of all believers who are convinced and convicted by the Holy Spirit. Rebekah has an enormous bride price paid for her, but notice that the paying of the price is *not* dependent on her answer. It was paid *before* she was asked if she would become the bride. She must make the decision for herself. The servant has given Rebekah a few gifts from Isaac, but as she becomes his wife she will possess everything that he has. Rebekah believes the servant and goes with him to meet her bridegroom in the field as he comes out to meet her in the evening.

For the Church/the Bride, our bride price was paid by Christ on the cross. Then as the Holy Spirit works, each individual makes the choice whether to go with Him becoming part of the Bride of Christ. Those who do are joined to Christ and become joint heirs with Him (Romans 8:17).

Notice Rebekah doesn't see Isaac until she marries him. As 1 Peter 1:8–9 tells us, "Though you have not seen him, you love him; and even though you do not see him now, you believe in him and are filled with an inexpressible and glorious joy, for you are receiving the end result of your faith, the salvation of your souls."

Isaac is a type of **Christ.** In this chapter we see Isaac coming from *Lahai roi*, "the living and the seeing one," the well that Hagar named when she met Christ there. He comes to the field in the evening to meet Rebekah and bring her home. It seems to be love at first sight, yet her face is veiled. It isn't her physical beauty overwhelming him. He has completely submitted to the will of God for his life, and God has already given him a love for her.

After being offered up as a sacrifice by His Father on the cross, Christ has risen from the dead. He is waiting in heaven where He is preparing for His wedding, when the bride will be brought to Him by the Holy Spirit. This picture is true to the Jewish culture and era: wedding processions were formed to go and get the bride and bring her to the groom's home—his father's house—where the wedding was to take place. Often the bride didn't know the date or time of her own wedding. It was a surprise!

Jesus Christ loved us while we were yet sinners, even though there was nothing in us to attract Him (Romans 5:6–8) and many things to repel Him. Notice that Isaac meets his bride in the field, which usually symbolizes the world, in the evening. When Jesus comes for His Church, the world will be in a time of spiritual darkness (Romans 13:11–12). Most of us see that all around us now. I've often wondered if, as this is pictured, the Rapture will take place literally in the evening—that as the sun goes down, the *Son* will come down.

One day, we'll see.

Chapter 7
Jacob, God's Struggler

I love the story about Henry Ward Beecher, a preacher who lived in the 1800s. (He was also the father of Harriet Beecher Stowe, the abolitionist author of *Uncle Tom's Cabin*.) One morning as he stepped up to the podium of Plymouth Church to preach, he found a letter waiting for him. He opened it and saw that it contained only one word: "FOOL."

With becoming seriousness, he announced to the church the contents of the letter. Then he said, "I have known many an instance of a man writing a letter and forgetting to sign his name, but this is the only instance I have ever known of a man signing his name and forgetting to write the letter."

Most of us have probably had times we felt like a fool—whether anyone called us one or not. But maybe that realization speaks well of us. As Shakespeare said, "The fool doth think he is wise, but the wise man knows himself to be a fool."

David Roper wrote a great little book with the title *Jacob: The Fools God Chooses*. But we'll see that title doesn't tell it all because Jacob's life story could also be titled—*Jacob: The Fools God Loves*. Occasionally, I could have substituted my name in that first title, and I assume that your name might fit just as well. The good news is that both our names also fit well in the second title because we are infinitely loved by God.

In this chapter, we're going to look at Jacob who acted foolishly many times in his life. Although he was in the line of Christ, he was *never* a type of Christ. But the pre-incarnate Christ did visit Jacob three times as recorded in Genesis 28, 32 and 35.

Jacob, the Schemer: Genesis 25–28
The marriage of Isaac and Rebekah is beautiful in Genesis 24—but then life happens. Here we look at them later in their lives, not as

spiritual types but as plain people with their faults fully on display. (I've often been grateful that God stopped writing the Bible almost 2,000 years ago so that my personal sins could never find their way into the Bible.)

Rebekah has been childless for 20 years with Isaac fervently praying for her to have children. For a moment, think of Isaac's father, Abraham. We may think that when the story moves on to the son, the father has died. But Abraham is still around. He lived 35 years past the time Isaac was married (25:7). Don't you imagine that he was also praying and maybe wondering why—once again—the hoped-for arrival in the promised line was being delayed? Barrenness: first Sarah and then Rebekah. It was, as Yogi Berra said, "déjà vu all over again." But as someone else said, "God is seldom early, but never late."

In God's timing Rebekah becomes pregnant, but it's a rough pregnancy with a lot of tumult going on inside her. When she asks the Lord about it, He gives her a divine ultrasound announcement: you're having twins.

Two nations are in your womb, and two peoples from within you will be separated; one people will be stronger than the other, and the older will serve the younger." When the time came for her to give birth, there were twin boys in her womb. The first to come out was red, and his whole body was like a hairy garment; so they named him Esau. After this, his brother came out, with his hand grasping Esau's heel; so he was named Jacob. Isaac was sixty years old when Rebekah gave birth to them (Genesis 25:23–26).

When the babies are born, it's obvious that they are fraternal twins—they don't look alike or act alike. The firstborn is called *Esau* or "red." His brother comes out holding onto Esau's heel as if he'd been trying to drag his brother back and put himself into the firstborn position. Isaac may have laughed as he named him *Jacob* or "heeler," which in Hebrew also meant "to deceive." It would be like naming a baby boy "Hustler" in our culture. Unfortunately, Jacob will live up to his name.

These children bring something besides joy into the marriage of Isaac and Rebekah. As the boys grow, the parents choose favorites. Isaac, a passive contemplative man, prefers Esau, his polar opposite. Esau is a strident man's man, a hunter of game. Rebekah chooses Jacob, a homebody who learns to cook. (This obvious parental favoritism has become a "don't do this" chapter in many Christian parenting books.)

Parental favoritism does in Isaac's home what it always does: it sets up a bickering, adversarial relationship between the parents and between the boys. They see the "Dad likes you better" "But Mom loves you more" thing happening, and they resent it. It's not an excuse for Jacob, but it may be part of the reason that he buys the birthright from Esau and later tricks him out of the blessing. Because his father prefers Esau, Jacob doesn't think he will do what the Lord had told Rebekah—and she no doubt had told Jacob—allow the older (Esau) to serve the younger (Jacob).

As we join Jacob's story in chapter 28, the background is that he has bought his older twin's birthright (25:29–34) for a bowl of stew. He made sure he was in the right place at the right time with what his brother would be craving after a long day of hunting. The one good thing that can be said of Jacob is he really *wanted* that birthright. All the more praiseworthy because it was not an inheritance of wealth; the majority of that would still go to the firstborn. The birthright was the right to participate in the covenant God made with Abraham. It was the right of *primogeniture.* The firstborn son was entitled to be in the line through which the Messiah was to come. It was a *spiritual blessing.* Esau saw no value in it and willingly sold it for almost nothing. When Esau sold it and Jacob bought it, God honored their deal: it was to be through the line of Jacob and his son Judah that Jesus Christ would come. (Remember, it was also the way God had said it was to be.)

Not satisfied with getting the birthright, Jacob also wants his father's blessing. His mother overhears Isaac planning to give it to Esau, so she helps Jacob disguise himself with some goat hair added to his arms. She provides a meal of fresh game fixed the way Isaac loves it. And Jacob lowers his voice to trick his old, blind father. Their plan works and Isaac gives the blessing to Jacob.

Isaac finds out what has happened when Esau brings in his own freshly-killed meal, ready for his father to bless him. But the blessing has been given and can't be retracted, even though Esau begs his father to do so. At this point Esau is fed up; he's ready to kill his brother. In the odd way of true stories, Esau often seems to be a better person than Jacob. Esau was like some people you may know, who although they are ethical and nice, are also *godless*. Esau cared nothing about God or spiritual things. Today the word for him would be *secular*.

Jacob has cheated and gotten what he wanted, but he knows that he won't be able to stay home and enjoy it. Although he certainly doesn't have a sterling character, it is the trickster Jacob that God has chosen the Messiah's line to come through. Because of Jacob's deception, God could have counted him unworthy and refused to be called Jacob's God. Instead, 25 times in the Bible He calls Himself "the God of Jacob."

Rather than waiting for God to change Isaac's mind, Rebekah and Jacob had tried to help God out, *to get His will their way*. Isaac discovered that he had been tricked into giving Jacob the blessing, but he also finally realized that Jacob was God's choice and that he had been defying God by trying to give the blessing to Esau. As chapter 28 begins, Isaac calls Jacob in and gives him a repeated blessing, this time fully conscious of what he's doing. He reminds him that he must marry a woman in the family line of Shem, not a Canaanite (line of Ham)—to keep the genealogical line of the coming Messiah in the family God chose.

Jacob, afraid of his brother and urged on by his mother, makes a run for it. When Jacob leaves, he's obviously really moving because a pedestrian could cover about 20 miles per day and he covered nearly 40. He was determined to put space between himself and Esau. Exhausted, he lies down to sleep and has a dream that is more than a dream. God directly speaks to Him from the "stairway" (not "Jacob's ladder"). David Roper in his book *Jacob* writes:

"What caught Jacob's attention, however, was not the stairway but the fact God was standing *beside* or *alongside* him, for that's the meaning of the preposition translated 'above' in verse 13. . . . What is important to visualize is that God had come *down* the ramp. The God of Jacob's father, Isaac, and grandfather, Abraham, was at his side in this desolate place, contrary to Jacob's expectations and far away from the traditional holy places he normally associated with God's presence."

In this passage, Christ is the stairway that links heaven and earth. In another of those instances where Jesus confirms His presence in the Old Testament, we see Jesus speak of this time as He calls a new disciple, Nathanael:

Then Nathanael declared, "Rabbi, you are the Son of God; you are the king of Israel." Jesus said, "You believe because I told you I saw you under the fig tree. You will see greater things than that." He then added, "Very truly I tell you, you will see 'heaven open, and the angels of God ascending and descending on' the Son of Man" (John 1:49–51).

We see a picture of the grace of God as the pre-incarnate Christ standing next to Jacob gives seven promises as to what He will do for Jacob. These are all part of the unconditional covenant that God had made with his grandfather Abraham.

As Jacob wakes up, he remembers each word and is suddenly aware of Lord's presence. He says, "Surely the LORD is in this place, and I was not aware of it." He was afraid and said, "How awesome is this place! This is none other than the house of God; this is the gate of heaven" (28:16–17). If you use the word "awesome" to describe things, there are relatively few places it should be used. This was one of them. Realizing the import of what has happened to him, Jacob changed the name of the place from Luz ("separated") to Bethel ("House of God").

Because Jacob had not yet gotten to the end of himself, he had not yet begun with God. The "fools God chooses" part comes in the way Jacob responds after being given assurances that the presence of God will go with him. Jacob answers these wonderful promises with, "If God will be with me and will watch over me on this journey I am taking and will give me food to eat and clothes to wear so that I return safely to my father's household, then the LORD will be my God and this stone that I have set up as a pillar will be God's house, and of all that you give me I will give you a tenth" (vv. 20–22).

Like most of us, Jacob has two sides to his faith. He erects a stone of remembrance and renames the place after God, which are acts of faith. But he also has a bargaining spirit in which he's looking to get whatever he can. The *hustler* says to God "if you will, then I will ..." He knows very little of the character of God. His highest thoughts of God's goodness were that He would keep supplying material things and physical protection. But, are our prayer requests much better? Do we often just pray for material possessions or health for ourselves and our family and friends, rather than for spiritual growth and the opportunity to be a blessing to others and further the growth of God's kingdom on earth?

Jacob, the Wrestler: Genesis 32
Emily Dickinson wrote:
> *"A little east of Jordan,*
> *Evangelists record,*
> *A Gymnast and an Angel*
> *Did wrestle long and hard."*

Although it makes a great poem, it wasn't an "Angel" who wrestled with Jacob (the "Gymnast") but the pre-incarnate Christ.

The background of the story happens in the chapters between Genesis 28 and 32. Jacob has been living with his mother's brother Laban's family for 20 years. He has married two of Laban's daughters, Leah and Rachel, and had children. He has worked for Laban managing his flocks and increasing his wealth, and he's found that Laban was as much of a hustler as he ever thought to be. In chapter 31 he sees that the relationship between himself and Laban and his sons is deteriorating. Then God tells him directly to go home (31:1–3). Rather than tell Laban directly that he's leaving, he "deceives Laban" (31:20), packs everybody up, and sneaks off. This causes a confrontation when Laban follows him—charging that he hadn't even let him say goodbye to his children and grandchildren.

After that confrontation, he has another one to face as he goes to make amends with his brother Esau. Genesis 32:7 tells us Jacob was in "great fear and distress." As Shakespeare said "conscience doth make cowards of us all." If anyone ever needed the help of God it was Jacob, and as the chapter opens he receives help; he is allowed to see that there are angels around him. He names the place Mahanaim, "two camps" because he realizes there is a spiritual camp surrounding his camp.

Jacob divides his family into two groups, sending them ahead, hoping to save at least half of them if his meeting with Esau turns violent. As it turns out, Esau is coming in peace with reconciliation in mind, but Jacob doesn't know that. In verses 9 to 12 we see the first recorded evidence of a desperate Jacob praying. It's come to that! Augustine wrote, "The best disposition for praying is that of being desolate, forsaken, stripped of everything." Jacob is all that. He's looking at possibly losing everything and he's crying "out of the depths" (Psalm 130:1). But he wisely bases his plea on the promises of God (which we too can claim), essentially saying "remember when You said . . ."

Since Jacob is a man on the edge, surely God will come to him with great gentleness and comfort. *No.* The pre-incarnate Christ does visit him, but not to comfort him. It's often said that "Jacob wrestled with the Lord," but really the Lord wrestled with Jacob to get something from him. Early on, Jacob realizes he is fighting with someone other than just a man. Why do they wrestle all night? Christ without lifting a finger could have subdued Jacob. Christ wrestles with Jacob like a man wrestles with his little son, not using a fraction of his strength but waiting until the child is worn out with the effort.

At the end, Jacob is holding onto Christ—he's figured out who it is—trying to wrestle a blessing from Him. Christ is holding onto Jacob until he gives up all that he has lived by: the pride and deceit. Finally, as dawn is about to break and Jacob hasn't given up, Christ shrivels the strongest sinew in his thigh, giving him a limp as a constant reminder of this night for the rest of his life.

F. B. Meyer wrote: "Our greatest victories are wrought through pain and purchased at the cost of the humbling of the flesh . . . the secret of prevailing with God and man [is] not in the strength, but in the weakness of the flesh." Jacob had to learn this and so do we.

There is a shift in Jacob's attitude overnight that will last the rest of his life. Jacob realizes he is no longer wrestling an unknown man to avoid being beaten. He knows that God is wrestling with him, and he is "holding on for dear life." Jacob never really says "I give." He says something better, "I will not let you go unless you bless me" (v. 26). Jacob has gone from fighting to clinging. He was learning a valuable lesson: we don't get anywhere with God by struggling and fighting; the only way is by yielding and holding on.

An elderly preacher said that when he was little and his mama got a switch and started to smack his legs with it, he learned a secret. Instead of trying to get away, he would hug her legs. The switching suddenly hurt much less as the blows were shortened and didn't have a sting.

Jacob has a change of attitude and, with it, he gets a name change. Christ says he will no longer be called "Jacob" or "Deceiver" but "Israel" which means "he *struggles* with God." Then Jacob names the place of this meeting, Peniel, which means the "face of God."

God wrestled with Jacob until the breaking of day. God crippled his mortal body to get to his immortal soul. But Jacob isn't the only combatant in history. God may have struggled with you or me for years about specific parts of our lives. When we are not willing to yield, He sometimes puts something out of joint: our bodies or our families or our plans. He does it—not to hurt us—but to get us to yield and cling to Him.

David Roper wrote of Jacob, "His maiming marked him forever. But if you were to ask about his infirmity, he would tell you that the best day of his life was the day God put him on the mat. That was the night Jacob lost everything he had and gained everything worth having."

Jacob, the Prophet: Genesis 49
Deathbeds are sometimes the place where things that needed to be said long ago are finally said—whether by the person dying or those gathered around. In biblical times there were no hospitals with IVs and drugs that could prolong death or keep the dying person sedated. People who died a natural death often were conscious, with their family gathered around them. For many, it became the last chance to think back over their lives and to settle things

At this point we'll abbreviate what happens to Jacob in many chapters in order to fast forward to his deathbed. What he says there directly relates to Christ, the Messiah to come.

After Jacob had met with God (Genesis 32), he buys some property and tries to settle down near Shechem. But soon his daughter Dinah is raped by the king's son (Genesis 34). Two of her older brothers, Simeon and Levi, take an uneven revenge by slaughtering all the men of the town and looting it. When told about it, Jacob seems more upset about his reputation and safety than about what happened to his daughter or how out of control his sons were. We see this as he wails that now people from surrounding areas will probably kill them all (34:30).

Donald Barnhouse wrote: "A man cannot be unfaithful without the results coming home to roost. Jacob had met God, had received great visions and blessings, had done many spiritual things; now, because of unfaithfulness he was to be brought low, even to great tragedy....Where Jacob was living it was good for his sheep but bad for his lamb." Barnhouse was talking about Dinah, but it was bad for all Jacob's lambs—all his children.

Spurred on by this fear of the neighboring people groups and told by God to move to Bethel, Jacob does. At this time he becomes serious about his relationship with God. He heads up a family revival (Genesis 35) and gets rid of the idols some of his family members had. He rededicates his life, and God protects his family by causing a rumored threat, the "terror of God," to fall on all the cities they pass by (v. 5).

At this point, Jacob takes his family back to Bethel where he had first met God on the stairway from heaven in chapter 28. He builds an altar and renames the place El Bethel, changing it from the "house of God" to the "God of the house of God." Here Christ appears to him again (35:9–10) and reminds him of his new name, Israel, and the covenant He had made with his grandfather Abraham and his father Isaac. Because of God's grace—not Jacob's faith or lack of it—that covenant is his too.

Although Jacob sets his house in order in some ways; other areas he doesn't touch. He does nothing about the rabid sibling rivalry among his sons. This will cause trouble until, in a rage, Joseph's brothers sell him into slavery. That action results in the whole family being relocated to Egypt years later. And it is there that Jacob, surrounded by his family, lies dying. Genesis 49 records the scene.

It's sad if you have to say of anyone that the time he or she behaved in the godliest way was on their deathbed, but this is what we see happening with Jacob. In fact, it's one of the few times God calls him *Israel*, which is his spiritual name. The blessings Jacob gives his sons are spiritually discerned and are prophetic of the future of the tribes each will father. A particularly prophetic blessing is that one son will be an ancestor of the coming Messiah/Christ.

Normally, the best blessing always went to the oldest son—but not in this case. Why did Reuben (49:3–4) not get this blessing? Reuben had slept with his father's concubine, who would have been the mother of some of his half-brothers. (What a mess polygamy can cause!)

The next two oldest sons also don't get this supreme blessing. Instead, Jacob pronounces a curse on Simeon and Levi: Although he didn't do anything to them at the time, on his deathbed he castigates them (vv. 5–7) for their cruelty to the inhabitants of Shechem after the rape of Dinah: "Simeon and Levi are brothers—their swords are weapons of violence. Let me not enter their council, let me not join their assembly, for they have killed men in their anger and hamstrung oxen as they pleased. Cursed be their anger, so fierce, and their fury, so cruel! I will scatter them in Jacob and disperse them in Israel."

Because the words were coming from God, each of the prophecies Jacob speaks concerning his sons come true. Simeon and Levi were scattered regarding their inheritance of land. Simeon's tribe shrank during the desert wanderings. When they got to Canaan, it was the smallest tribe and was allotted cities inside Judah's boundaries. Eventually the tribe melded into Judah. Because Levi was the priestly line, they were to inherit no land but live in the boundaries of the other tribes. Notice the grace of God in making Levi's line priests after what he did.

If you and I could choose our ancestors we would probably choose the wisest, best-looking, and most godly people in each generation. Jesus had the choice, and He chose some individuals who were godly and some who were mired in sin. In other words, He chose to come from people just like our ancestors. After Jacob's oldest three sons disqualify themselves, his fourth son, Judah, becomes the direct ancestor of Jesus. Judah fathered twin boys by his former daughter-in-law (this sordid tale is in Genesis 38). And the younger twin, Perez, shows up in the line of Christ (Matthew 1:3). Although Judah is certainly no example of virtue, he will receive the Messianic blessing spoken of in Genesis 49:8–10:

Judah, your brothers will praise you;
  your hand will be on the neck of your enemies;
  your father's sons will bow down to you.
You are a lion's cub, Judah;
  you return from the prey, my son.
Like a lion he crouches and lies down,
  like a lioness—who dares to rouse him?
The scepter will not depart from Judah,
  nor the ruler's staff from between his feet,
until he to whom it belongs shall come
  and the obedience of the nations shall be his.

In verse 10, we see the name "Shiloh" in some versions. This refers to the Messiah. It is translated here "until he to whom it belongs shall come" because the word Shiloh means "whose it is." This "it" refers to the "scepter" or right to rule.

Each tribe of Israel would later have a symbol or logo displayed on the flag that would mark their tribe's area when they encamped in the wilderness. The symbol of the tribe of Judah is of a lion (the king of beasts) lying down with a scepter between his feet—taken straight from this prophecy.

Who would be foolish enough to try to take a scepter out from between the feet of a fierce lion? Often in Scripture, Jesus is spoken of as the Lion of the tribe of Judah. This reminds us that, although Jesus was meek and lowly in His first coming, He won't be in His second coming. In keeping with this prophetic personification in *The Chronicles of Narnia,* C. S. Lewis portrayed the Christ-figure *Aslan* as a huge lion. Children can ride on him and pet him, but he is fierce with enemies. And as Mr. Beaver says, "He is not a tame lion, but he is *good.*"

Chapter 8
Joseph, from the Pit to the Palace

For a number of years Broadway hosted performances of *Joseph and the Amazing Technicolor Dreamcoat*. With such poles-apart personalities playing Joseph as rock singer Andy Gibb of the Beegees and pop singer Donny Osmond, the production must have some universal appeal. From the snippets I've seen on *youtube*, it varies from the biblical story significantly. Each of Joseph's eleven brothers has a large letter—the first initial of his name—on his shirt. I don't know if that is to help the audience or the actors keep their names straight. And there's a lot of singing and dancing. The real story of Joseph doesn't have any singing and dancing that we know of; nevertheless, it's quite a remarkable one. Especially when you consider that it covers about a third of the book of Genesis. In the last 14 chapters of Genesis, Jacob's name (including his new name *Israel*) appears 62 times, but Joseph is mentioned 133 times.

Although there are many examples of Joseph being a *type of Christ*, there are a number when he first comes into view in Genesis 37:

1. The birth of Joseph was miraculous in a way because it came as an answer to prayer. Jesus' birth was certainly miraculous.
2. Joseph was especially loved by his father. Jesus was loved by His Father who declared, "This is my beloved Son."
3. Joseph had a special coat which showed he was the heir. Christ was shown to be the Son and heir of the Father by many miraculous signs. All who come to Him are joint heirs with Him.
4. The brothers ridiculed Joseph's dreams that seemed to say he would rule over them. Jesus was ridiculed,

especially as He hung on the cross where a sign above Him proclaimed mockingly, "King of the Jews."
5. Joseph was hated by his brothers without a cause. (The dreams he told them about imply nothing wrong on his part; he simply told them what he had dreamed.) Jesus was hated by His brethren (the Jews) without a cause.
6. Joseph's father sent him to find his brethren. God the Father sent Jesus to seek and to save His brethren.

With all these similarities to Jesus and the fact that no evil is spoken of him, it's easy to see why G. Campbell Morgan wrote of Joseph: "no more remarkable figure appears on the pages of Old Testament history."

A Type of Christ as Savior: Genesis 37–50

Joseph's birth is first mentioned in Genesis 30:24. His mother Rachel gives him a name which means, "May the Lord add to me another son." Since this is her first child it seems odd naming a child "just the first one" but it's probably an act of gratitude for finally having a son. (She will have another son but will die in childbirth as he, Benjamin, comes into the world.)

As a young child, Joseph sees jealousy and fighting among Jacob's two wives and two concubines. Then his mother Rachel dies while he is still young, and he watches his father grieve deeply for her. Joseph becomes his father's favorite child—a reminder of the woman he loved. Even though Jacob's family seems to have put the "funk" in "dysfunctional," Joseph emerges as a 17-year-old boy with a sterling character. That's where we begin the story of his life in Genesis 37.

Of all the characters in the Old Testament, none show us the purpose of God more clearly than Joseph. But, for all his faithfulness, Joseph is one patriarch to whom *God did not appear* directly. While we look at Joseph as a perfect type of Christ, notice that's he's also a perfect type of what the New Testament believer should be. We too have not seen God. He has not appeared to us (1 Peter 1:8–9) and yet we are asked/expected to live by faith. Joseph shows us how it can be done, even in the worst of circumstances.

There are no New Testament verses we can quote that are proof texts for calling Joseph a type of Christ. Only two places mention him: Acts 7:9–14 and Hebrews 11:21–22. But there are so many parallels between Jesus and Joseph that it's hard to avoid that conclusion.

As a type of Christ: remember what Jesus asked the two walking with Him on the road to Emmaus: "Did not the Messiah have to suffer these things and then enter his glory?" (Luke 24:26). Joseph also had a lot of suffering in his life.

There are more personal details given about Joseph than any other character in the Bible. We see the hand of God working again and again to fulfill His purposes. In his life as a believer, Joseph represents the testing and triumph of faith. Joseph brought a bad report about his brothers to his father—not because he was a snitch but because they were *bad guys*. His brothers were almost like gang members, and it wasn't long between problem behavior breakouts. Their father apparently thought he'd better watch over them in case they decided to wipe out the men of another city and loot it as they had done to Shechem in Genesis 34. Jacob knew he could trust Joseph to bring him a true report.

Jacob had chosen Joseph to be the heir both because of his love of Rachel and because the firstborn sons of the other three mothers of his children had proven unworthy of trust. As mentioned in the last chapter, Genesis 35:22 tells us that Reuben slept with one of this father's concubines. Because of this, the birthright was taken away from Reuben, the eldest of Leah's sons, and given to Joseph, the eldest of Rachel's sons. Although Joseph had nothing to do with this displacement, the brothers hated him for this too.

Joseph was shown to be special by the (literally) "long-sleeved robe" Jacob had made for him. The NIV says it was richly ornamented. *The Message* says it was embroidered. Traditionally, Bible story books for children have called it "many-colored." Regardless of what it looked like, it was intended to show Joseph was special—he was the chosen heir. Unfortunately, Jacob was repeating the preferential treatment he'd seen his own father give his twin brother Esau. Now Joseph was the recipient of that favoritism, as well as Benjamin.

How did the other brothers react? They hated Joseph because he was the father's favorite and his true report had brought down their father's wrath on them. They also envied him; he was good and honorable and they weren't.

As a type of Christ: Why did the Jewish leaders want Jesus crucified? Even Pilate could see it. In Matthew 27:18 he said that it was because of envy they wanted him killed. Jesus' purity held up a mirror to their evil.

Nothing sinful or wrong is ever recorded about Joseph. Even in telling about his dreams he wasn't bragging; he was telling the truth. God gave Joseph the dreams to prepare him for his future. Joseph told his family about them because the dreams fascinated him, and he probably didn't imagine such a simple thing could provoke hatred. The brothers used the dreams as an excuse to escalate their jealousy and anger. The dream about the moon and stars bowing down to him enraged them and even upset Jacob (vv. 9–11).

Joseph showed great humility—the dreams didn't puff him up and didn't make him live in fear of his brothers. He trusted God with his life and didn't fear others. At the request of his father, Joseph left home and sought his brothers who were out with the flocks (just as Christ left His heavenly home to seek and save His brethren). After traveling 40 miles to Shechem, Joseph finds out that they've gone to Dothan. This will make the trip about 100 miles. It also shows the irresponsibility of the brothers who may have been out looking for excitement. They shouldn't have been moving that far or that fast. You don't drive sheep like cattle; you let them graze where there is enough grass.

The brothers begin to plot the minute they see Joseph in his distinctive coat coming in the distance. The original plan is murder, but Reuben intercedes. This is amazing when you consider that Joseph has been given Reuben's place as the heir. Nevertheless, he tries to save Joseph. When he returns from being away and finds that the brothers have sold him (v. 29), Reuben truly grieves.

The brothers take Joseph's special coat and throw him into a dry well. This was a preamble to murder. They were going to leave him there until they worked up the nerve to kill him. Then they just calmly sat down to eat—possibly food that Joseph had brought them—while they could hear him crying out to them for mercy. They showed a callousness that they will remember and regret when the tables are turned.

Suddenly, the brothers have a different idea (no doubt given by God who was not going to let Joseph be killed). *"Wait—we could make money on this!"* Judah suggests. Joseph brings 20 pieces of silver as he's sold to a Midianite caravan passing by.

As a type of Christ: Jesus never did any wrong yet some hated Him and plotted to get rid of Him. He was sold into the hands of the chief priests and Pharisees by Judas for 30 pieces of silver. (The lives of both Joseph and Jesus were valued at a slave's price.) The Pharisees delivered Christ to be crucified and tried to get it done quickly so they could go home and eat the Passover. And even as Jesus was dying on the cross, the soldiers gambled at its foot to win Jesus' special seamless coat that a follower lovingly made for Him.

At first it looks like Joseph's sale in the slave market in Egypt lands him in a good place (Genesis 39). He is bought by Potiphar, Pharaoh's captain of the guard, and treated well. As Joseph works faithfully, Potiphar sees that the Lord is with him and promotes Joseph to run his whole household. Then Potiphar's wife tries to seduce the handsome young man. He flees from her.

Enraged, she grabs his cloak and tells her husband that Joseph tried to rape her. Potiphar probably knew better but had to side with his wife to save face. Rather than killing him as he could have, he throws Joseph in prison.

Even in prison Joseph excels. The warden puts him in charge of the whole prison "because the Lord was with Joseph and gave him success in whatever he did." Still, he hoped to be released after interpreting dreams for Pharaoh's cupbearer and baker and having them come true. He asked the cupbearer to remember him and to help get him released after he was restored to his position in three days. The cupbearer promised, but forgot (40:23).

Joseph was tested in many ways and spent 13 years in slavery and in prison. But God is not locked out of prisons (no matter what our prison is). In the 1600s John Bunyan was a tinker in England who became interested in religion. He joined a non-conformist group and became a preacher. Bunyan was arrested and spent 12 years in jail because he refused to give up preaching. Much of *The Pilgrim's Progress*, one of Christendom's greatest classics, was written while Bunyan was incarcerated in Newgate Jail.

Maybe Bunyan and Joseph occasionally wondered why God didn't get them out of prison because they were innocent of any crime. Why did the cupbearer, who owed Joseph, forget him? Looking at the whole story with the beauty of hindsight, we know the timing wasn't right then. Pharaoh probably would have rewarded him by sending him home. But Joseph was needed in Egypt at the time Pharaoh had his dreams, so he had to stay in prison two more years. When Joseph interprets Pharaoh's dreams of the upcoming famine, he is in one day catapulted *from the prison to the palace*. Pharaoh makes him second in command of Egypt to prepare for the famine, and he becomes the savior (from starvation) of that part of the world.

Then he begins to understand God's plan. His 13 years of trials and sufferings are all in the plan of God who "called down famine on the land and destroyed all their supplies of food; and he sent a man before them—Joseph, sold as a slave. They bruised his feet with shackles, his neck was put in irons, till what he foretold came to pass, till the word of the LORD proved him true" (Psalm 105:16–19).

Jesus, because He was God, knew God's plan and understood why He suffered, but it was, nonetheless, suffering. He was many times bone weary. He went without food 40 days at least one time. He suffered in daily life and then endured the ultimate suffering on the cross for us. Hebrews 5:7–9 says:

During the days of Jesus' life on earth, he offered up prayers and petitions with fervent cries and tears to the one who could save him from death, and he was heard because of his reverent submission. Son though he was, he learned obedience from what he suffered and, once made perfect, he became the source of eternal salvation for all who obey him.

The Tables Turn: Genesis 42–45

God has overruled events to bring Joseph to this point: through the brothers' jealousy, the slave caravan, the lust of Potiphar's wife, the forgetfulness and then remembrance (at the perfect time) of the cupbearer from prison, the dreams of Pharaoh, the faith of Joseph, the wisdom of Pharaoh to put Joseph in control, the bountiful harvests for seven years, the storage of surplus, and the beginning of seven years of famine. God has put Joseph in the right place at the right time as only He can do.

The region-wide famine also strikes the land of Canaan. Jacob hears there is food in Egypt and sends the ten brothers, keeping (his new favorite) Benjamin at home. I wonder if the brothers thought about what they had done to Joseph as they traveled the same road to Egypt that the Midianite caravan would have taken him. Something they say later indicates they had all lived with considerable guilt. Donald Barnhouse wisely wrote: "The word

Egypt in their ears must have sounded like the word *rope* in the house of a man who has hanged himself."

When the brothers arrive, Joseph recognizes them immediately even though about 22 years have passed (42:6–8). But they have no clue that he is their brother and not an Egyptian. Racially, the pharaohs of that day were not the dark-skinned Egyptians we think of today. With the black wig he wore and the eye makeup (used to deflect the bright sun off their eyes like sunglasses), Joseph would have been pretty much unrecognizable. He will take advantage of that and wait for the right time and place to reveal himself. The Egyptians weren't obligated to sell food to foreigners. The brothers find themselves in a position lower than slaves—they are essentially beggars. Joseph, by withholding who he is from his brothers, is going to test them. They'd massacred a village and sold their own brother into slavery, which they assumed was a death sentence. Have they changed?

As a type of Christ: Remember that Jesus did not come into His public ministry announcing that He was the Messiah. And to some, who figured it out, He told them to keep quiet about it. This section reminds us that Jesus "was in the world, and though the world was made through him, the world did not recognize him" (John 1:10).

Joseph has total power over whether his brothers live or die. If he wasn't merciful, if he hadn't forgiven them, he could have them killed—or sold into slavery, in an eye-for-an-eye fashion. (For that matter, he could have taken revenge on Potiphar's wife and had her killed or imprisoned, but he didn't.) He knows his brothers, but they still don't know him.

When the brothers tell about themselves they count Joseph as having been one of them. "Your servants were twelve brothers" they say, rather than "we are eleven brothers." It shows he has been on their minds. Knowing how hard the lives of slaves were, maybe they assume he died young. They certainly couldn't imagine that he stands before them.

Joseph begins a series of tests to see if they are changed men. He sends them home with their money in their sacks of grain. They pass the honesty test by returning it and bringing more money the next time they come to buy food.

His final test will show if they are willing to abandon another brother. He has Simeon put in jail until they return with the youngest brother, Benjamin, to free him. Joseph undoubtedly knows how hard it will be for Jacob to let Benjamin out of his sight, so this test for the brothers will be the hardest.

Because Joseph was speaking to them through a translator, they feel safe in speaking to each other in Hebrew. When they speak about being punished for what they did to Joseph, he turns away to keep them from seeing his tears. They recall how Joseph cried out to them and how they ignored his pleas.

As a type of Christ: Joseph had brothers who should have helped him but turned their backs on him. Now think about those who were like brothers to Jesus. When He was arrested, the disciples fled. Peter followed afar off and then denied even knowing him. Of the twelve, John stayed as close as he could get to Him until the end at the foot of the cross, joining some of His faithful women followers.

When the brothers do come back with double the money and Benjamin, Joseph still doesn't disclose who he is. He invites them to another meal and seats them in their exact birth order (43:33). This astounds them.

In Genesis 44 their money is once again returned in their sacks when they leave, but Joseph's silver cup is put in Benjamin's sack. They're pursued, searched, and brought back as thieves. Joseph pretends to be ready to enslave Benjamin, but Judah makes an impassioned plea for his life. He offers to stay as Joseph's lifetime slave if Benjamin is returned to his father.

As a type of Christ: Although Judah's offer to substitute himself is not accepted, his earthly descendent, Jesus, will become the ultimate Substitute and give His life for all who accept His sacrifice.

In Genesis 45:1–15 we see Joseph, finally convinced that his brothers have changed and unable to withhold the knowledge of who he is any more. He sends everyone out but the brothers. Then in a very tender scene he reveals himself saying, "But God sent me ahead of you to preserve for you a remnant on earth and to save your lives by a great deliverance. So then, it was not you who sent me here, but God." This is similar to what he will tell them years later when, after their father's death, they fear he may yet take revenge on them: "You intended to harm me, but God intended it for good to accomplish what is now being done, the saving of many lives" (Genesis 50:20).

As a type of Christ: God the Father sent Jesus Christ the Son to people who would die in our sins without the deliverance He alone could bring. One day Christ will come again and reveal who He is to his earthly brothers, the Jews, who rejected Him at His first coming. Revelation 1:7 says: "Look, he is coming with the clouds," and "every eye will see him, even those who pierced him"; and all peoples on earth "will mourn because of him."

When the brothers return and tell their father Jacob what has happened, they also have to confess what they did to Joseph. Jacob believes them (the text at that point calls him "Israel" because he is acting in faith). At Joseph's invitation, the whole family will move to Egypt to be with Joseph and will be treated well.

It's interesting to notice that the message the brothers gave their father is like the message we have for the spiritually starving world today: *The One who saved us is alive. He is exalted and He wants to receive you.*

Chapter 9
Moses, the savior and Jesus, the Savior

Imagine the great leader Moses lived today and applied for the job of managing a government agency responsible for the oversight of two million people. If, through personal connections, he got an interview with the president's chief of staff, can you imagine that conversation?

Chief of Staff: Mr. Moses, I see that you were reared by our most prominent family and have an MBA from a prestigious school. After that, you were put in a position over a large staff in your first job and stayed there about 17 years. Why did you leave that position?

Moses: I saw one of my supervisors abusing a worker and intervened. Let's just say I handled it decisively, but my boss—who was a relative of my adoptive mother—took the other side of the matter. That's when I decided it would be best to relocate.

Chief of Staff: [writes "quick-tempered"] Well, executive jobs can have their stresses. Your résumé says that you then worked as "Chief Shepherd" for a man named Jethro. You do have quite a tan and look like an outdoorsman.

Moses: Yes, after I moved to a rural area, I met my wife. Her father needed someone to manage his flocks. Even though animal husbandry wasn't my field, management is management. I helped increase his bottom line considerably. Sheep in many ways are like people. You might be surprised at the similarities.

Chief of Staff: Uh-huh [writes "jobs by nepotism"]. By the way, the dates don't seem to be here. How long did you work for . . . your father-in-law?

Moses: For the last 40 years.

Chief of Staff: [Does some quick addition in his head and writes, "80 YEARS OLD!" He stands up and extends his hand.]

Thank you so much for coming in, Mr. Moses. You understand that we have other candidates to interview, but we'll certainly let you know something soon. [*When hell freezes over*, he thinks.]

This modern illustration shows that even though Moses became a deliverer/savior to his people, he might not have looked—then or now—to anyone (except God) like a good choice. Many commentators have pointed out that Moses' life of 120 years divides up evenly into thirds. He spent the first 40 years in Egypt as a prince in a palace and the second 40 years in the wilderness as a shepherd tending flocks for his father-in-law. His final 40 years he spent in the wilderness tending the children of Israel, who were far more stubborn than any sheep. As D. L. Moody said: "Moses spent 40 years thinking he was a somebody, 40 years learning he was a nobody, and 40 years finding out what God can do with a nobody."

When the Book of Genesis closed, Jacob's family consisted of 70 people who were being well treated in Egypt because their son/brother was second in command of the country. But about 400 years later as the Book of Exodus opens, things have changed considerably. The descendants of Jacob have multiplied to possibly two million people. Somewhere along the way, a pharaoh took over who didn't know or care that Joseph had saved the country. In the time-honored tradition of despots, he took advantage of controlling a large immigrant population, which native Egyptians disliked anyway, and enslaved Jacob's descendants.

The rulers of Egypt wanted cheap labor to build their treasure cities and elaborate tombs, but they also were afraid that the swelling ranks of Hebrews might someday revolt. One pharaoh decided to stop the Hebrew population explosion by killing all the male children. Some godly parents risked their lives to save their children. As Hebrews 11:23–28 shows, Moses' journey of faith began with the family he was born into:

By faith Moses' parents hid him for three months after he was born, because they saw he was no ordinary child, and they were not afraid of the king's edict. By faith Moses, when he had grown up, refused to be known as the son of Pharaoh's daughter. He chose to be mistreated along with the people of God rather than to enjoy the fleeting pleasures of sin. He regarded disgrace for the sake of Christ as of greater value than the treasures of Egypt, because he was looking ahead to his reward. By faith he left Egypt, not fearing the king's anger; he persevered because he saw him who is invisible. By faith he kept the Passover and the application of blood, so that the destroyer of the firstborn would not touch the firstborn of Israel.

Or as Vance Havner succinctly put it in an overview of his life of faith: Moses was able to "see the invisible, choose the imperishable, and do the impossible."

Types and Shadows
In the Pentateuch, we see various types of Christ, from a lamb to manna to a rock to a place of worship. But Moses was also a *type of Christ* because he was the deliverer of his people. When the children of Israel cried out to God in their misery, He sent them a savior with a small "s." Notice some similarities between Moses and Jesus:

Moses the savior and Jesus the Savior both began life as babies who had to be rescued from vicious kings who ordered all the Hebrew boy babies killed (Exodus 1:8–22; Matthew 2:13–18).

Born to a poor slave couple, Moses only escaped death when his mother placed him in a basket and hid him in the bulrushes of the Nile. Pharaoh's daughter found him, adopted him, and took him to live in her palace, making him essentially the future ruler of Egypt, the most advanced civilization in the world. Jesus was born to Mary and Joseph, a poor couple, but Jesus' true father was God. When an angel warned Joseph of King Herod's plans to kill all the male babies and eliminate a future rival, he and Mary took baby Jesus to

Egypt to keep Him safe. Ironically, He who was born King of kings, never lived in an earthly palace.

Moses and Jesus each grew to full maturity before the time was right for them to deliver their people. However, the typology was interrupted when Moses was about 40. He tried to deliver one of his people by taking matters into his own hands and killing an Egyptian who was abusing a Hebrew (Exodus 2:11–12). Jesus, on the other hand, never killed anyone or sinned in any way. Instead, He gave sight to the blind, healed the sick, and raised the dead.

After Moses killed an Egyptian, he knew that Pharaoh would be out for revenge. He fled into the desert where he spent 40 years. As someone said, there he got his BS—backside of the desert degree. And there, the *pre-incarnate Christ* appeared to him and spoke to him through a burning bush. Although the Speaker is called "the angel of the Lord," the first-person references show this was far more than an angel (Exodus 3:2–6):

There the angel of the LORD appeared to him in flames of fire from within a bush. Moses saw that though the bush was on fire it did not burn up. So Moses thought, "I will go over and see this strange sight—why the bush does not burn up." When the LORD saw that he had gone over to look, God called to him from within the bush, "Moses! Moses!" And Moses said, "Here I am."

"Do not come any closer," God said. "Take off your sandals, for the place where you are standing is holy ground." Then he said, "I am the God of your father, the God of Abraham, the God of Isaac and the God of Jacob." At this, Moses hid his face, because he was afraid to look at God.

Moses became the savior of his people but, unlike Jesus, he was a reluctant savior. He first argued that he wasn't capable of talking to Pharaoh but finally agreed to go. God said that his brother Aaron could do the talking, but we never see that happening.

Apparently, Moses found his tongue. He was given the power to summon miraculous plagues and prove that the "let My people go" message came directly from God. Because God was with him, Moses was able to lead the children of Israel out of bondage.

Frederick Buechner in *Wishful Thinking* compared Jesus to Moses when he wrote: "On the other hand, [Jesus] not only went further than Moses, but claimed his own to be the higher authority. Moses was against murder. Jesus was against vindictive anger. Moses was against adultery. Jesus was against recreational sex. Moses said love your neighbor. Jesus said love your enemy too. Moses said be good. Jesus said be perfect (Matthew 5:21–48)."

Like a Lamb: Exodus 12
Through the plagues, Moses showed Pharaoh the mighty power the real God had over his imaginary gods of nature. Because of Pharaoh's stubbornness, the country of Egypt was nearly destroyed. The worst plague was the last which culminated in the death of every firstborn including Pharaoh's son, his heir to the throne. Finally, Pharaoh was broken and ready to let the children of Israel go.

Before the last plague that would cause Pharaoh's change of mind, God prepared a tradition to show His people—in type—what redemption would look like. The head of each family was to kill a lamb and apply its blood to the doorways. The death angel would "pass over" those households while striking each Egyptian household. The Passover became for Jews the touchstone of their faith. A memorial that represented God's love for them and their redemption from slavery. They have kept this annual celebration for thousands of years.

Why did God use a lamb? If I wanted to picture the gentlest baby animal, I wouldn't use a kitten or even a puppy (kittens can scratch and puppy teeth are sharp). I'd use a lamb because a lamb has no aggressive tendencies. It also has no claws or sharp teeth to accidentally bring harm. With this gentle creature, God taught the children of Israel that redemption was not free; it came at a price.

The instructions for choosing and preparing the Passover lamb are given in Exodus 12. Verse 3 says that each family was to choose a lamb to sacrifice. If the family was too small to eat a whole lamb, neighbors were to be brought in. However, a lamb was *never* too small for the household. One lamb would be sufficient. Remember when John the Baptist pointed to Jesus and said, "Behold! The Lamb of God who takes away the sin of the world" (John 1:29 NKJV). His sacrifice was sufficient to atone for *all* the sin of the world past and present.

Even though we think of a lamb as a baby animal, the lamb had to be a year-old full-grown male (Exodus 12:5). It had to have no known blemishes or defects. As Peter wrote, "For you know that it was not with perishable things such as silver or gold that you were redeemed from the empty way of life handed down to you from your ancestors, but with the precious blood of Christ, a lamb without blemish or defect" (1 Peter 1:18–19).

The lamb was to be chosen on the tenth day of Nisan, the first month of the Jewish religious calendar, and kept up for *four* days (Exodus 12:3, 6). It was probably brought into the house. And if there were children . . . you know they would become attached quickly. The lamb was killed on the fourteenth day of Nisan because, no matter how sweet and gentle the lamb was, it was only through its death that people could be saved from the death plague. All four gospels tell us that Jesus was questioned and tested repeatedly in the days before Passover (John 13:1; 18:28). At no time were his enemies able to trip him up or prove any defect in Him—because he had none. He asked the Jews in John 8:46, "Can any of you prove me guilty of sin?"

The lamb had to be roasted, not boiled, so the meat would not separate from the bones (Exodus 12:8). To be a type of Christ's sacrifice, the lamb must be whole. Going through the fire to be roasted symbolizes Christ going through the fire of God's judgment. All of it was to be eaten. Any meat left over had to be burned (vv. 9–10). Because it was highly symbolic, it was not treated like ordinary food. It didn't become sandwich meat for the trip into the desert. In the salvation Christ provides, you can't pick and choose cafeteria-style, as some try to do.

The lamb's blood put on the doorpost was a sign of faith in the promise of redemption (vv. 12–13). God said, "when I see the blood, I will pass over you." The promise of (physical) salvation was clear but, to access it, the heads of each Jewish household had to *apply* the blood. Anyone who wouldn't obey because it was too simple or they felt it was beneath them would put a death sentence on his firstborn. There is no biblical record of any Israelites refusing to participate. They desperately wanted to be freed from their bondage.

The paschal lamb was to have no bones broken (Exodus 12:46). When Jesus was on the cross, soldiers came to break His legs as their custom was to speed the dying process. But they realized He was already dead, they didn't break His legs (John 19:36). The soldiers probably thought they were just being practical, but God had foreordained that none of the Lamb of God's bones would be broken. As the psalmist wrote, "He keeps all his bones; not one of them is broken" (Psalm 34:20 ESV).

New Testament writers tell us that the lamb is a picture of Christ in several ways. But Paul made the Exodus 12 connection crystal clear when he wrote in 1 Corinthians 5:7 that "Christ, our Passover lamb, has been sacrificed."

In the Cloud and Fire: Exodus 13

The children of Israel had given Moses a hard time when he first came to Egypt from his self-imposed exile. They doubted his claims that God was about to free them from their slavery and use him to lead them out. But, as he performed each God-directed miracle and the resolve of pharaoh crumbled, it became apparent that God really had sent Moses. Unfortunately, that didn't mean the people never again balked at his leadership. Even family members took their shots. Later God says directly to Moses' sister and brother, who criticized him over his remarriage after he was widowed (Numbers 12:6–8), that Moses was unlike almost every other leader:

"When a prophet of the LORD is among you, I reveal myself to him in visions, I speak to him in dreams. But this is not true of my servant Moses; he is faithful in all my house. With him I speak face to face, clearly and not in riddles; why then were you not afraid to speak against my servant Moses?"

Moses, God's servant, had a unique relationship with God. But the people often forgot that. What they could less easily forget were the direct, visible signs of the leading of the Lord. "By day the LORD went ahead of them in a pillar of cloud to guide them on their way and by night in a pillar of fire to give them light, so that they could travel by day or night" (Exodus 13:21).

The people might have thought they were following Moses, but they were really following Moses following Christ, who was constantly present with them. The wilderness had no signposts or streetlights, but the children of Israel had something far better. Christ graciously provided a cloud to partly shade them by day and a pillar of fire at night to keep them from stumbling in the darkness.

Between the Devil and the Deep Red Sea: Exodus 14

This heading was a Chuck Swindoll message title on Moses who, thru God's power, parted the Red Sea and led the people through on dry ground. Then the sea surged back in and drowned the Egyptians who tried to pursue them. Notice verse 19 where the angel of God (Christ) in the pillar of fire moved from in front of them to behind them, putting Himself between them and their enemies. Verse 24 tells us the Lord was in the pillar of fire and cloud. He threw the armies of Egypt into total confusion, jamming their chariot wheels. Even the Egyptians understood that it was the Lord fighting against them and for the Israelites (v. 25).

Paul especially wanted to make sure his people, the Jews, understood how much symbolism there was in the deliverance from Egypt and the wilderness journey of the children of Israel and how much in it speaks—to Jew and Gentile—of Christ: "For I do not want you to be ignorant of the fact, brothers and sisters, that our ancestors were all under the cloud and that they all passed through the sea. They were all baptized into Moses in the cloud and in the sea" (1 Corinthians 10:1–2).

Did you notice that they were "baptized into Moses in the cloud and in the sea" and no one even got wet? This baptism has nothing to do with water; it is a picture of their identification as God's people. Moses paints a beautiful picture of their complete deliverance. They are on their way to the Promised Land, led by Christ Himself. So everything will be great from now on, right? Well, not exactly.

Their Daily Manna: Exodus 16
As the children of Israel go through the wilderness, we see them repeatedly grumble against Moses and the Lord (16:2). Imagine complaining that your life was better when you were a slave! But as someone said about complainers, "For some people there's nothing quite like their former pastor or their first husband (or wife)."

Charles Stanley said that with God's help it was fairly easy for Moses to get the people out of Egypt, but getting Egypt out of the people was another matter altogether. For them to complain—when they were visibly and constantly being taken care of by God—seems incredible to us. Until we remember how often we complain, even though we are incredibly blessed and eternally freed from the slavery of sin and the fear of death.

Although the Israelites had been delivered from slavery and death and were guided by the presence of God in a cloud by day and a pillar of fire by night, they grumbled. They became afraid they would starve. At that time, they probably still had some food they had brought with them; a miraculous delivery of food hadn't been necessary. (God never does miracles when a natural solution is available.) But they weren't patient. They talked about going back to slavery in Egypt—for the food (v. 3)!

We don't usually think about complaining as being sin, but it is. Maybe that's why Paul wrote, "Do all things without complaining and disputing" (Philippians 2:14 NKJV). The NIV translates it "grumbling or arguing." Paul could have been thinking of the Israelites of the past or believers in his own time. Complaining essentially is saying that I resent the place and circumstances that the Lord has me in, and I know better than He does. As someone said, grouchiness is a sin against love. (*Ouch!*)

No matter what the Israelites might have believed, the Lord didn't bring them into the wilderness to let them starve. He created a never-before-seen food with all the vitamins needed to maintain their health—*manna*. The word for manna in Hebrew translates to "What is it?" Probably because that's what the Jews said when they first saw manna covering the ground like a fresh blanket of snow. It appeared every morning except the Sabbath. They were told to gather twice as much on the day before the Sabbath because they weren't going to get any on the Sabbath. Otherwise, they were not to try to save it but to collect it daily, showing that they were depending on the Lord to provide more each day.

As usual, some people thought they knew better than Moses (v. 20). They tried to save some manna from one day to the next. But, as they had been told, the next day it was covered with maggots and stank up their tent.

Manna was provided every day for 40 years until they entered the Promised Land and could eat the crops of the land. It's been estimated that to feed that large a crowd (two million +), the manna for even one day would have filled 10 railroad trains that had 30 boxcars each with 15 tons in each boxcar. There is no way that number of people could have survived 40 years in a barren desert without God supernaturally feeding them.

The manna in Moses' day kept the physical bodies of the Israelites alive. Today receiving Jesus as our manna, our Bread of Life, means that we will live eternally with Him. There are at least seven ways in which manna was a type or picture of Christ:

1. It came down from heaven.
2. It was a supernatural gift of God.
3. It was given at night.
4. It came to where the people were.
5. It was pure and small. (Jesus came in a humble way.)
6. It was sent when Israel was about to perish.
7. It either had to be gathered and eaten or walked upon/rejected.

In John 6 Jesus described Himself as the Bread of Life. After He had fed the five thousand, Jesus crossed over to the other side of the Sea of Galilee. The crowd showed up the next day hoping to have their stomachs filled again. They tried to goad Him into duplicating the miracle of the manna—after all it provided ample food and lasted 40 years—but He told them there was a more lasting and important bread available:

So they asked him, "What sign then will you give that we may see it and believe you? What will you do? Our ancestors ate the manna in the wilderness; as it is written: 'He gave them bread from heaven to eat.'" Jesus said to them, "Very truly I tell you, it is not Moses who has given you the bread from heaven, but it is my Father who gives you the true bread from heaven. For the bread of God is the bread that comes down from heaven and gives life to the world."

"Very truly I tell you, the one who believes has eternal life. I am the bread of life. Your ancestors ate the manna in the wilderness, yet they died. But here is the bread that comes down from heaven, which anyone may eat and not die. I am the living bread that came down from heaven. Whoever eats this bread will live forever. This bread is my flesh, which I will give for the life of the world."

God provided food and water for the Israelites in the wilderness to sustain them physically. But there was a much deeper meaning. As Paul wrote, "They all ate the same spiritual food and drank the same spiritual drink; for they drank from the spiritual rock that accompanied them, and that rock was Christ" (1 Corinthians 10:3–4).

If you're still looking for proof texts, here is another from Paul: "that rock was Christ."

Chapter 10
Moses and the Lawbreakers

Everyone who has seen the classic 1956 film *The Ten Commandments,* starring Charlton Heston, has a favorite part. I have several. One is the crowd scene leaving Egypt when thousands of Middle-Eastern looking extras got work for a day or two. The people, camels, and donkeys stretched for as far as the eye could see. Director Cecil B. DeMille narrated the film himself, telling of the "mixed multitude" that came out. In the film (not in the Bible) that even included Moses' Egyptian adopted mother.

There's that dramatic moment when the newly-freed people were screaming because they saw in the distance the Egyptian army pursuing them. Heston/Moses shouted, "Stand still and see the salvation of the Lord." Then he stood on a rock above the Red Sea, stretched out his staff toward the sea, and yelled, "Behold His mighty hand." A wind blew and the waters started rolling back. For not having computer animation to work this miracle, the film makers did a remarkable job giving a sense of it. However, what took the strong east wind all night to do was accomplished Hollywood-style in less than a minute.

Another scene showed Moses on Mt. Sinai with God (a dazzling fireball) while God wrote the Ten Commandments on the stone tablets by hurling fireballs at them. When Moses came down from the mountain with the tablets, he heard a lot of noise from the camp. Coming closer, he saw the people dancing around a golden calf—a scene as idolatrous as any in the pantheistic Egypt they'd just left. DeMille solemnly intoned, "The people rose up to play and did eat and drink and were as the children of fools. . . ." In a rage, Moses threw down the tablets and broke them.

Although this movie version was a lot closer to the Bible account than movies made in later years would be, it did change some of the details by melding two events into one. Moses tells us that the people had been in the wilderness three months and were encamped at the base of Mt. Sinai when God first gave him the Law verbally (Exodus 19–23). God came to the top of Mt. Sinai in a thick, dark cloud and met with Moses. The people were kept behind a barrier at the base of the mountain. They didn't want to get any closer! Even at a distance, the trembling mountain, the lightning, and loud trumpet blasts terrified them. The writer of Hebrews used this to compare the difference between them being under law and New Testament believers being under grace (Hebrews 12:18–19, 21):

You have not come to a mountain that can be touched and that is burning with fire; to darkness, gloom and storm; to a trumpet blast or to such a voice speaking words that those who heard it begged that no further word be spoken to them, . . . The sight was so terrifying that Moses said, "I am trembling with fear."

Later Moses would, at God's invitation, go up the mountain again. Exodus 24:3–4 says,

When Moses went and told the people all the LORD's words and laws, they responded with one voice, "Everything the LORD has said we will do." Moses then wrote down everything the LORD had said. . . .

After making sacrifices for the people, "Moses and Aaron, Nadab and Abihu, and the seventy elders of Israel went up and saw the God of Israel. Under his feet was something like a pavement made of lapis lazuli, as bright blue as the sky. But God did not raise his hand against these leaders of the Israelites; they saw God, and they ate and drank. The LORD said to Moses, 'Come up to me on the mountain and stay here, and I will give you the tablets of stone with the law and commandments I have written for their instruction'" (Exodus 24:9–11).

Notice that it was not just Moses who "saw God" but 73 other people also saw Him. (This appearance, I believe, would also be the pre-incarnate Christ, because He is the One who deals personally with us on earth.) This was probably done to give Moses plenty of backup witnesses for what he would tell the people when he gave them the Law. The people could never say all this was the dreams or delusions of one man—as many cults have been based on what one person saw or dreamed.

The next morning Moses went up on the mountain to meet with the Lord and to receive the tablets of stone with the abbreviated law on them (Exodus 24:12). A cloud covered the mountain and Moses went into it. He stayed on the mountain with God 40 days and 40 nights. At this point, the Bible account leaves Moses on the mountain for seven chapters and details how the tabernacle and its furnishings are to be constructed (Exodus 25–31).

In chapter 32 the story of Moses picks up again. During the 40 days Moses was gone, the people got nervous and decided he wasn't coming back. They said to Aaron, "Come, make us gods who will go before us." And Aaron did it, melting down the gold jewelry they contributed. By the next day, they were in full party mode around the golden calf (32:6).

God knew exactly what was going on at the foot of the mountain. He told Moses that He was getting ready to destroy this "stiff-necked people" (32:9–10) and start over with Moses. But Moses interceded for the people. He asked God to remember His covenant with Abraham and not destroy them. God agreed. He carried the two tablets, written by God, down the mountain. When Moses saw what was going on, he was so irate that—as Heston demonstrated—he threw the tablets down and broke them. (God would later make him another set.)

Although God did not destroy the nation, there was a price to pay. Moses had the gold calf ground to powder and made the people drink it in their water. He also asked the men who were on his side to take their swords and kill those involved. Three thousand died that day.

God had graciously redeemed the people out of Egypt and slavery and provided for them for 40 years in the wilderness, this golden calf disobedience was just the start of what would be a long disobedience.

Water from the Rock: Exodus 17
The people were grumbling *again*. Moses cried out to God that they were almost ready to stone him (Exodus 17:4). God told him to take his staff to the rock at Horeb, strike it, and water would come out. He did and water flowed from the rock.

Here the rock is a type of Christ because He was struck—died on the cross—for us and from His death we received living water. Remember what Jesus said in John 7:37–39:

On the last and greatest day of the festival, Jesus stood and said in a loud voice, "Let anyone who is thirsty come to me and drink. Whoever believes in me, as Scripture has said, rivers of living water will flow from within them." By this he meant the Spirit, whom those who believed in him were later to receive. Up to that time the Spirit had not been given, since Jesus had not yet been glorified.

The Israelites complained about water at the beginning of their journey and, 40 years later, at the end they were still complaining (Numbers 20:1–13). At that time, Moses became so frustrated with them that, instead of speaking to the rock as the Lord instructed him that time, he disobeyed and struck it—twice. Possibly worse is what he said: "Must *we* bring you water out of this rock?" as if claiming part of the glory for what was done. The rock that provided life-giving water was a type of Christ, therefore the striking only had to happen once. We're told not to, by our disbelief, crucify Christ again because He "died to sin once for all" (Romans 6:10; also see Hebrews 7:27; 9:26–28). This was a costly error on Moses' part.

Because of his disobedience, God told him he would not be able to enter the Promised Land.

Moses named the place "Massah" which means "to test" and "Meribah" which means "quarreling." Whenever they spoke those names, he wanted the Israelites to remember what happened there and to learn from it. Unfortunately, history doesn't record that they did.

The Bronze Snake: Numbers 21

Snakes—the things nightmares are made of! Years ago a *rattle* near the feet of my horse set off a life or death runaway ride through the New Mexico desert. By the time we stopped, I don't know whose nerves were in worse shape—mine or the horse's. I learned a valuable lesson that day about how dangerous snakes are in the desert.

As the children of Israel traveled through the wilderness—a desert—they didn't necessarily have to tangle with snakes. God was protecting them from all their natural enemies until . . . they started complaining again. Then God used snakes to punish the people for their repeated disobedience and ingratitude (Numbers 21:4–9):

They traveled from Mount Hor along the route to the Red Sea, to go around Edom. But the people grew impatient on the way; they spoke against God and against Moses, and said, "Why have you brought us up out of Egypt to die in the wilderness? There is no bread! There is no water! And we detest this miserable food!" Then the LORD *sent venomous snakes among them; they bit the people and many Israelites died. The people came to Moses and said, "We sinned when we spoke against the* LORD *and against you. Pray that the* LORD *will take the snakes away from us." So Moses prayed for the people. The* LORD *said to Moses, "Make a snake and put it up on a pole; anyone who is bitten can look at it and live." So Moses made a bronze snake and put it up on a pole. Then when anyone was bitten by a snake and looked at the bronze snake, they lived.*

The people were grumbling again—about almost everything, including the manna which has been described as "angel's food." The Lord chastened them by sending snakes among them to bite them. But, with the punishment, He also gave a way for the people to be healed and live. God told Moses to make a bronze snake and put it on a pole. Since it would be very difficult to hang even a bronze snake on a pole, it's likely there was a crosspiece on the pole over which the snake was hung. If so, it would be a *cross* that the snake was draped over. Although the last thing that snake-bitten people wanted to look at was a replica of a snake, those who obeyed Moses and looked were healed.

Jesus explained His connection to this incident as He was talking about the new birth and saving faith one night to Nicodemus who, as a Pharisee, knew this story very well. Jesus told him, *"Just as Moses lifted up the snake in the wilderness, so the Son of Man must be lifted up, that everyone who believes may have eternal life in him"* (John 3:14–15).

Since the Garden of Eden, the snake has been a symbol of sin. By comparing Himself— although perfect and holy—to a snake, Jesus was giving Nicodemus a look several years into the future when He was to be lifted up on the cross and "made sin for us" (2 Corinthians 5:21). And all who looked to Him could be healed of the plague of sin.

A Place of Refuge: Numbers 35
The Law of Moses is often pointed to as being merciless in its application, such as in the eye-for-an-eye laws. There was certainly a reason for this. Israel of old didn't maintain jails or appeals courts or have people on death row for 20-plus years as America does. Penalties were swift and corresponded to the crime. If you intentionally murdered, you would be executed. If you committed a white-collar type theft, you would be required to pay back the victim a much larger amount than you had stolen. (Charles Colson

advocated for this in his prison ministry.) What seems harsh to some was a system that kept crime to a minimum and punished evil-doers quickly.

But there also was mercy in the Judaic system. God had Moses set up six "cities of refuge," three on each side of the Jordan and scattered throughout the country for easy access. These were the remedy provided for unintentional killing (Numbers 35:22–23). The relatives of a slain person had the right of blood vengeance but, after a trial by the leaders of the congregation (Numbers 35:12, 24–25; Joshua 20:4), a killing could be found to be accidental or unintentional. In that case, the one who had killed had the right to go to one of the cities of refuge. This would ensure his safety from those who might want to kill him. Essentially, going to a city of refuge meant he was throwing himself on the mercy of God and accepting His provision. However, there were restrictions. The accused would have to stay in that city; if he ventured out, he was fair game. He couldn't leave the city of refuge for any reason until the high priest died. Then he was free—similar to a presidential pardon.

In the city of refuge, we see Christ pictured in two ways: He is our city of refuge—the one we run to because we are sinners (born so) even if we never intended to be. But He is also pictured in the high priest, who by his death set free all who had previously been secluded in a city of refuge. As in many types of Christ, every detail isn't exact. For instance, the cities of refuge were not for those who had committed premeditated murder, but Christ is our refuge and the expiator of sins that were done either intentionally or unintentionally—once we have truly repented of them.

Glimpses of Grace
Dr. Richard Swenson in *More Than Meets the Eye* wrote, "What we need is a new vision of God. The real God. Not some vague image we fold up and stuff in the back drawer of life, but the kind of God who parts the Red Sea and shakes Mount Sinai. The kind of God

who stuns the physicians with symmetry, the mathematicians with precision, the engineers with design, the politicians with power, and the poets with beauty."

We often think of Old Testament saints as having very little knowledge of the ways of God compared to believers on this side of the Cross. But, even under the Law, there were some beautiful pictures of God's love and grace. It just takes looking a little deeper than we often do. These pictures eventually find their fulfillment in Jesus Christ. But still we don't see it all. At least, not yet.

The Message paraphrases 1 Corinthians 13:12: "We don't yet see things clearly. We're squinting in a fog, peering through a mist. But it won't be long before the weather clears and the sun shines bright! We'll see it all then, see it all as clearly as God sees us, knowing him directly just as he knows us!"

Chapter 11
Christ in the Tabernacle and the Offerings

For ten years I worked as a real estate agent showing many buyers prospective houses. I also sold some houses in new subdivisions where the buyers' house would be built from the ground up to their taste. Buyers were both stressed and excited as they watched their houses progress day by day. I remembered how excited my husband and I were when we bought our first house in the process of construction and could make even a few choices. I learned more of what my clients were feeling when my husband and I decided to build a "spec" (on speculation) house. It was a house contracted with a construction company to be built purely for resale. I had to find a house plan that we could afford to build, that would fit well on the grade of the lot, and that would maximize the view of a lake across the street.

Although I've made many choices in our own houses and houses we've rehabbed over the years, this was the most difficult. I knew it didn't matter much if the floor plan, light fixtures, appliances, and finishes in the house were to my taste. What mattered is if they would appeal to buyers. To recoup our investment, the house needed to appeal to many people, not sit on the market waiting for just the right person. Thankfully, when it was *finally* finished, it sold quickly. But the process was extremely stressful and produced so little profit that we vowed never to do it again.

Maybe it's because of my background in real estate that when the Bible describes the construction of something, such as the tabernacle or the temple, I don't skip over that section. Yes, dimensions and material descriptions can seem boring but, I remind myself, God had a purpose in telling us these details. And I've found there's often a deeper, symbolic meaning to even these sections.

Although God doesn't live in—isn't confined to—a house of worship, He made it clear that after the Jews constructed these "houses," first the movable tabernacle and later the immense limestone temple, His presence would inhabit them.

The House that God Built
Tim Keller, a well-known pastor and author in New York City, once tweeted: "Jesus is the Temple to end all temples, the priest to end all priests, and the sacrifice to end all sacrifices."

Similarly, Jesus was the tabernacle to end all tabernacles because the temple built in Jerusalem by Solomon (and later rebuilt by Ezra and Herod) was simply the larger and more permanent form of the tabernacle. The function and the furnishings were the same.

Here is a diagram of the later built temple which shows the basic parameters and boundaries which had to be observed by lay people and by priests. Any Jewish man could go through the two outside courts (Gentiles and Women) to get to the Court of the Men, but he was not allowed to go into the Court of the Priests unless he was both a priest and had been chosen by lot to do service at that time. A woman could go through the Court of the Gentiles to get to the Court of Women but could not go into the Court of Men. There were no women priests. Gentiles who were interested in the faith could go no farther than the Court of the Gentiles.

God gave Moses the instructions for the tabernacle (and temple) offerings and he recorded them in various places in the Pentateuch. The main instructions for the tabernacle are in Exodus chapters 25–40, and the main instructions for offerings are in Leviticus.

Exodus is a book of deliverance which talks about the redemption of the children of Israel. Leviticus is a book of purification which talks about their sanctification. The overall way in which Christ is foreshadowed or shown in type in these two books follows that same theme: The Israelites were delivered from certain death at the hands of the Egyptians. After their physical deliverance, God set up a system for them to worship Him daily and live as His redeemed earthly people. The parallel is that through Christ's death on the cross, we have been saved—a one-time act—delivered from eternal death. Through His sacrifice and the subsequent gift of the Holy Spirit's presence in us, we are a redeemed heavenly people who are being sanctified daily—a lifetime process.

The Temple Complex

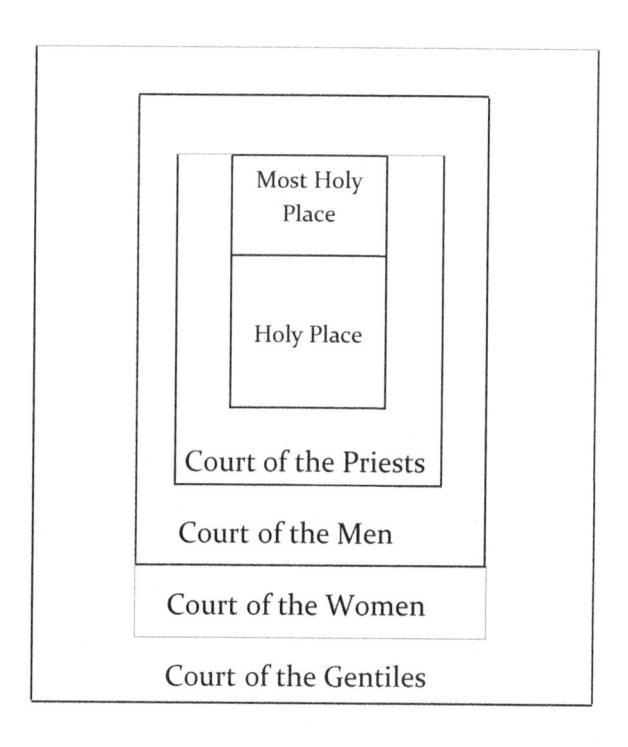

Most Holy Place
Holy Place
Court of the Priests
Court of the Men
Court of the Women
Court of the Gentiles

Christ in the Tabernacle: Exodus 25–30

Every building of any complexity starts out with plans or blueprints. Exodus 25–31 was the blueprint for the tabernacle and Exodus 35–40 included the construction project. This portable temple portrayed Christ both generally and specifically in many ways.

The tabernacle was a tent that looked like a larger version of the tents Israelites lived in. Now think about Jesus. John 1:24 says that Jesus "dwelt" among men, a word which literally means "pitched a tent." When He was born as a baby, He took on the same kind of external appearance as other human beings. Isaiah 53:2 says, "He had no beauty or majesty to attract us to him, nothing in his appearance that we should desire him." In other words, He didn't come into the world looking like Hugh Grant or Tom Selleck. There was no halo around His head in the manger or later—despite how medieval artists painted Him. Neither (we can be pretty sure) did He look like the beautiful *blonde* Jesus in a famous painting. He would have looked like a normal swarthy Jew of that time. No one could have merely looked at Him and said, "Obviously, this is God incarnate." But Colossians 2:9 says that was the case: "For in Christ all the fullness of the Deity lives in bodily form."

You've heard the expression, "It's what's inside that counts." That was especially true in the tabernacle. Its exterior was not awe-inspiring. The gold furnishings and exquisite beauty were reserved for the inside (which only the priests saw). The courtyard was a large linen-fenced area 75 feet wide by 150 feet long—about the size of two basketball courts. The tabernacle itself was the tent inside it and measured 15 feet wide by 45 feet long. It was divided into two sections by a heavily embroidered curtain or veil. The Holy Place which the priests entered daily was 30 x 15 and contained three pieces of furniture, while the Holy of Holies at the back end was 15 x 15 and contained only the Ark of the Covenant.

Specifically, each article of furniture or detail typifies Christ in some way. Even the order in which the six furnishings were set up within the linen fence has a meaning. If you had x-ray vision and an aerial view, you would see that the line of furnishings starting from the bronze altar outside and going into the Holy of Holies formed the shape of a perfect cross.

The tabernacle had a roof or covering that was made of four thicknesses of material (Exodus 26). The top covering was badgers' skin (a kind of seal abundant in the Nile and the Red Sea). It was a dull blue-gray, an unattractive but waterproof covering. The layer under that was the skins of rams dyed red (which symbolized blood). The third layer was goat hair. The goat was often a sin offering. But when the priest looked up, it was the fourth or bottom layer he would see: linen embroidered with beautiful cherubim in blue, purple, and scarlet.

A man in that day entered the gate taking his animal for sacrifice, but he did not go any farther. He slit the animal's throat and gave it to the priest who offered it on the bronze altar. Then the priest washed the blood off himself in the laver behind the altar. Morning and evening the priest on duty entered the Holy Place, the first compartment of the tabernacle, to keep the light burning in the golden candlestick on the left and burn incense on the golden altar of incense directly in front of the curtain which separated the Holy Place from the Holy of Holies. Once a week he changed out the 12 loaves of "showbread" on the table on the right.

The sixth piece of furniture was only seen once a year and only by one man. On the Day of Atonement the high priest went through the embroidered curtain into the Holy of Holies. He sprinkled blood from the sacrifice on the mercy seat of the ark of the covenant where the presence of God dwelt. Tradition says that because only the high priest could enter the Holy of Holies, the Jews worried that if something happened and he died in there no one would be able to get his body out (they couldn't go in without dying themselves). The people tied a long rope around his ankle with bells on it. If the bells stopped sounding for an extended period, they could drag the body out with the rope. Apparently, no priest succumbed and they never had to resort to that.

Parts of the Tabernacle
1. **The door or gate** of the outer tent was the only way in. The fence said, "Keep out," but the door said "Come in." The one

entrance showed that there is only one way to God. "I am the door," Jesus said in John 10:9.

2. **The bronze altar** was 7 ½ feet square and 4 ½ feet high and made of brass (Exodus 27:1–8). The fire on the altar was kept burning continually because there was no permanent payment for sin at that time. All animal sacrifices looked forward to the time that Christ would come and be the once and for all offering. "And by that will, we have been made holy through the sacrifice of the body of Jesus Christ once for all" (Hebrews 10:10).

3. **The laver** (Exodus 30:17–21) was probably a large washing vessel. The size is unspecified but it needed to hold plenty of water because it was used daily and extensively. It was made from the highly polished brass mirrors that women used. It shows that purification or cleansing is needed for us to be in God's presence. If a priest entered the tabernacle without washing his hands and feet, he would die. When priests were originally consecrated, they bathed all over and put on the sacred garments. After that, the only public washing was of the hands and feet. When Jesus washed His disciples' feet in John 13:1–10, He distinguished between being washed all over and needing only to wash their feet. As His disciples they were clean (saved), but walking through the world they would become defiled and need to come to Him through confession and repentance for cleansing (1 John 1:9). And the same is true for His followers today.

4. **The golden candlestick,** which was lit by oil, not by candles, had seven branches beautifully wrought out of pure gold and hammered into shapes like almond blossoms. (This menorah is not to be confused with the more modern and non-biblical nine-branched menorah used to commemorate Hanukah.) The golden candlestick was the only source of light in the Holy Place and was kept burning continually. It would have been extremely dark without it because of the heavy

coverings that made up the tabernacle. There is no indication that the Holy of Holies had any light. But "God is light and in Him there is no darkness at all." God said He would dwell above the mercy seat, so we can be sure the high priest would not have stumbled around in the dark in the Holy of Holies. The candlestick reminds us that Jesus is "the light of the world" (John 8:12).

5. **The table of showbread or the presence** held 12 loaves of unleavened bread which the priests changed out for fresh loaves weekly. It was the bread of the presence or literally "bread of faces." The 12 loaves probably represented the 12 tribes. Instructions for the bread were given in Leviticus 24:5–9. The priests ate the past week's loaves starting each Sabbath. Jesus said of Himself, "I am the bread of life" (John 6:48).

6. **The golden altar** on which incense was burned morning and evening represented the prayers of the people. It reminds us intercession is needed for God's people daily, not just on special occasions. "I pray for them," Jesus said in His great high priestly prayer (John 17:9). Since His resurrection, this ministry hasn't ceased. He is today at the right hand of God the Father interceding for us.

7. **The curtain between the Holy Place and the Holy of Holies** showed that there was separation between God and His people. Sin always separates us from Him. The writer of Hebrews tells us what this curtain symbolized: "by a new and living way opened for us through the curtain, that is, his body" (10:20). The huge curtain created later for the much larger temple has been described as being 60 feet high and 4 to 6 inches thick. It was so heavily embroidered that it was said two oxen pulling on it from opposite directions could not have torn it. Yet when Jesus died on the cross—the moment He gave up His spirit—the curtain in the temple was torn from the top to the bottom by the hand of God (Matthew

27:51). This signified the way between man and God was now open. Many priests who saw the torn curtain later believed in Jesus. Although the Jews tried to have the curtain repaired, the tear could not be mended.

8. **The Ark of the Covenant** was positioned behind the curtain and was the only furnishing in the Holy of Holies. The chest portion of it (about 4 feet long and 27 inches high) contained the tables of the Law, a pot of manna, and Aaron's rod that budded. The gold mercy seat had gold cherubim on each end and their spread wings overshadowed the ark. This was where the high priest would place the blood on the Day of Atonement (Leviticus 16). It points to the fact that only blood can make atonement for sin and that Christ is our mercy seat, the propitiation for our sins (1 John 2:2).

9. **Even the materials and colors** used in the tabernacle speak of Christ in symbolism used elsewhere in the Bible: the wood = His humanity; the gold = His divinity; white = His purity; blue = promise; purple = royalty; red = blood. There is no black in the tabernacle because black represents sin.

10. **The priesthood** shows that God had to be approached through representation. The writer of Hebrews talked about this (Hebrews 6:19; 7:27; 9:25; and 10:20 among other places):

Aaron As Priest	Christ As Priest
Entered the earthly tabernacle	Entered the heavenly temple
Entered once a year	Entered once for all
Entered beyond the veil	Tore the veil
Offered for his own sins	Offered for our sins
Offered the blood of bulls	Offered His own blood

Christ in the Offerings: Leviticus

In the past, in my well-intentioned attempts to read thru the Bible in a year, I often broke down at Leviticus. I either hurried through it or skipped it (after getting behind on the schedule) because I had no clue what it all meant. I figured if it was just instructions for the Jews about how to do their offerings—and they aren't doing that anymore—that it might be like the previous version of a current phone book. Until I studied it, I didn't know why it is still relevant. One of the reasons is because of the types of Christ in it.

Leviticus 1–7 explains five different kinds of offerings. The first three were voluntary; the last two were compulsory. The first three were offerings of dedication (Godward) and the last two were an atonement for sins. Notice that in each of these offerings, the details of how to handle it were explicit. This may be a reminder that God is not an any-old-way-will-do deity; He told those in the Old Testament days exactly how to come to Him through offerings. In the New Testament, He tells us that the one way is Christ and no one can come another way (John 14:6).

1. **The Burnt Offering** (Leviticus 1:1–9) was offered every morning and every night. It was usually a bull, although five male animals without defect were acceptable for this sacrifice, depending upon the financial state of the offeror: bull or ox, sheep, goat, dove and pigeon (vv. 10–17). The smaller animals and birds were offerings for poorer people. It was to be wholly consumed; the priests could eat none of it. The offeror had to bring it voluntarily and identify with it by putting his hand on the animal's head while killing it. In each case the offering, done in faith, is said to be "an aroma pleasing to the Lord." It is a picture of Christ as the patient, obedient Servant who was "obedient unto death" and who laid it all on the altar, holding back nothing.
2. **The Grain Offering** (Leviticus 2; 6:14–18) was a bloodless offering in which part of the baked or unbaked, but always

unleavened, offering was burned as a memorial portion on the altar—again "an aroma pleasing to the Lord" (v. 2). The rest of the offering was food for the priests. The grain offerings with their fine flour and no leaven, because leaven symbolizes sin, spoke of Christ and His sinless humanity, mixed with oil (the Holy Spirit), who went through the fires of degradation and suffering so that those in the priesthood (the New Testament says that is all believers) could feed on Him. It was to be offered every morning and evening with the burnt offering.

3. **The Fellowship or Peace Offering** (Leviticus 3) involved a bull, sheep or goat which could be male or female but always without defect (v. 6). The final verse of this chapter (v. 17) was to become part of the dietary laws of the Jews: they were to eat no fat or blood in their meat. Even today for meat to be "kosher" for Orthodox Jews, the blood is always completely drained, and an inspection done by a rabbi assures compliance. This was a festive offering because the meat was shared by the priests, but the offeror also received back part of it for his own sustenance. It is intricately linked to the burnt offering which pictures the cross because the peace offering was burned on top of the burnt offering (v. 5). It reminds us that Christ is our peace and that His work for us on the cross secured our peace *with* God (Romans 5:1) and allows us to have the peace *of* God in our lives (Philippians 4:7). Oddly enough to us, there is a prominence given to *fat*; God says *all* the fat is His (Leviticus 3:16). This is another "aroma pleasing to the Lord" offering (v. 5). The burning of fat certainly sends up more smoke and scent than lean meat does. A certain breed in that area was called a "fat-tail sheep." It had a tail that could weigh up to 15 pounds. A good choice for the peace offering!

Next we take up the two mandatory offerings which were definitely **not** "aroma pleasing" offerings:

4. **The Sin Offering** (Leviticus 4) has instructions that are repetitive to include each person or group—including leaders—who committed unintentional sin (there is never a sacrifice provided in the Old Testament for *intentional* sin). The instructions started with those for a priest who had sinned, then the whole congregation, next a ruler, and last a common individual. In each case after the sacrifice, the assurance is given that the offeror "will be forgiven." This offering had some parts burned on the bronze altar, but most of the carcass was considered corrupt (because it represented the essence of sin). It was taken outside the camp and burned in a ceremonially clean fire. In the era that Jesus was crucified, Jews insisted that criminals be killed outside their city gates so as not to "pollute" Jerusalem. That's why it was on a hill *outside* the walls of Jerusalem that Jesus—although perfect—was "made sin for us" (2 Corinthians 5:21). Someone said that the burnt offering tells who Christ is; the sin offering tells us what Christ did.
5. **The Trespass Offering** (Leviticus 5:1–6; 7:1–8) was described as a penalty or guilt offering (5:6). Unintentional sins or trespasses, once realized, required public confession, a blood sacrifice, and restitution. The restitution required repaying what had been defrauded or destroyed and adding 20% more to it. Here sin is looked upon as an injury done to someone. This reminds us that Christ restored what He hadn't taken away. He not only paid for our sins, He made us children of God, blessed us with all spiritual blessings, caused us to sit in heavenly places (Ephesians 1), and gave us the hundreds of blessings we have on this side of the Cross.

Christ, the Coming Prophet: Deuteronomy 18

Deuteronomy 18:15–18 says:

The LORD your God will raise up for you a prophet like me from among you, from your fellow Israelites. You must listen to him. For this is what you asked of the LORD your God at Horeb on the day of the assembly when you said, "Let us not hear the voice of the LORD our God nor see this great fire anymore, or we will die." The LORD said to me: "What they say is good. I will raise up for them a prophet like you from among their fellow Israelites, and I will put my words in his mouth. He will tell them everything I command him."

In this chapter and the previous one, we have looked at Moses as the savior of his people, the one who received the Law from the hand of God and the human author of the Pentateuch, but we rarely think of Moses as a *prophet*. We reserve that designation for men later in the history of Israel, men who foretold the future. Nevertheless, because prophecy is not just *foretelling* things in the future but *forthtelling* the Word of God, Moses was a prophet. He spoke for God to the people. In that way, Moses foreshadowed the One who was to come. The One who would literally be The Prophet—the voice of God—Jesus Christ. He would tell the people everything His Father commanded Him. As John 1:1 tells us, He was with the Word and He was the Word.

PART II
HIS STORY IN HISTORY

Chapter 12
The Jesus Joshua Knew

I am directionally-challenged. It's no secret in my family. That verbal "take a right at the second light and the next left and a right after that and you can't miss it" doesn't work. I will miss it. Invariably. And please don't tell me that it's simple. My mind doesn't work that way. I can google an address and print off and follow the written instructions (not a map). But the problem with those instructions is that you can't just reverse them for the return trip. There are often one-way streets, a different route to get back on an interstate, and other confusion-causing issues. And don't get me started on *detours*!

So, having this lifelong handicap, imagine my amazement when I found a cure. Really, our kids did. They gave my husband and I an anniversary gift of a portable GPS. The first time I suction-cupped that thingy to the windshield and typed in a local street address, I was amazed. It not only knew where I was, it knew how to get me where I wanted to go! And the female voice we had chosen to direct us wasn't nearly as irritating as a previous rental car's built-in GPS that had screeched at us each time we got off the trip route to eat, "No, turn around." "At the first chance, turn around." And almost shouting: "TURN AROUND!"

I first tested my new GPS on a trip to the gym because for that 11-mile trip, I knew where I was. But it worked just as well when we took a 500-mile trip and had to wind around the streets of Savannah in the dark. I felt like singing, "I once was lost but now am found."

Detoured

When people first hear that the children of Israel were in the wilderness for 40 years after they left Egypt, they may think they were lost. Israeli Prime Minister Golda Maier used to quip that

Moses wandered around Israel for 40 years and managed to settle in the only place where there was no oil. Cute, but not correct! At least, not about the wandering.

The children of Israel weren't *wandering* around lost with no GPS. Nor were they looking for black gold, Texas tea, or any other treasure. The normal 11-day journey took that long because God put them in a 40-year desert time-out after they initially refused to go in and take the land the Lord was giving them.

The number "40" in the Bible is often symbolic of the number of testing. In the case of the exodus, 40 years was the time it took a generation to die out. The generation that directly disobeyed God's command. God said that no one over 20 years old (the age a man could fight in the army) would be allowed to go into the land. Although the whole nation was punished for the sin of some of them, the children who had been 20 and under when they came out of Egyptian captivity could enter the Promised Land. God did not hold the disobedience of their parents against them.

One of the most beautiful examples of the love of God is that, although He was disciplining the people, He also continued to provide for them. He fed them and gave them water. Deuteronomy 8:4 says that during those four decades their clothes didn't wear out and their feet didn't swell. This indicated they had a nutritious diet and weren't susceptible to scurvy or other diet-related diseases.

Even Moses didn't get off unscathed. He had disobeyed too, although in a different way from the people (Numbers 20:7–12):

The LORD said to Moses, "Take the staff, and you and your brother Aaron gather the assembly together. Speak to that rock before their eyes and it will pour out its water. You will bring water out of the rock for the community so they and their livestock can drink."

So Moses took the staff from the LORD's presence, just as he commanded him. He and Aaron gathered the assembly together in front of the rock and Moses said to them, "Listen, you rebels, must we bring you water out of this rock?" Then Moses raised his arm and struck the rock twice with his staff. Water gushed out, and the community and their livestock drank.

But the LORD said to Moses and Aaron, "Because you did not trust in me enough to honor me as holy in the sight of the Israelites, you will not bring this community into the land I give them."

Part of Moses' sin in striking the rock instead of speaking to it to bring forth water was simple disobedience, but the more serious part was taking God's glory to himself with his "must *we* bring you water out of this rock?" Because of this, God told Moses he would not be allowed to enter the Promised Land.

Before he died and God buried him (Jude 9), Moses—at God's instruction—appointed his assistant, Joshua, to lead the people into the land. This began a new period in the history of Israel and a new book, *Joshua*. Moses, who wrote the first five books of Scripture, was dead; God raised up a new leader and a new author.

Joshua Takes the Lead
Joshua had been born and raised in Egypt and was about 40 at the time of the exodus. Redemption was personal to him. Think about it: as the firstborn son, Joshua's life had been the one spared in his family when the death angel passed over houses that had blood on the lintels of the door.

Joshua and Caleb had been two of the original 12 spies sent into the land when the Israelites first approached the border. Of the spies who gave their report to Moses, only two were in favor of going in to take the land. Because the people accepted the majority report instead of obeying God, the Israelites had to wander in the wilderness until that generation died out. However, God rewarded faithful Caleb and Joshua by letting them be the only two of their contemporaries to enter the Promised Land.

An apprentice to Moses for 40 years, Joshua was 80 when Moses died and he took over as the leader. But as someone said,

"When the man of God dies, nothing of God dies." Besides being a good and faithful man, Joshua was a type of Christ in many ways. Just a few are:

Joshua was named *Hoshea* which means "salvation." Because Moses knew the One who really saves, he renamed him *Joshua* which means "Yahweh saves" (Numbers 13:16). The angel of the Lord told Joseph to name God's Son "Jesus" (Matthew 1:21), which is the same as Joshua, because **Jesus** would "save his people from their sins."

Joshua led his army and destroyed the Lord's enemies. **Jesus** will lead His armies in the Battle of Armageddon in a massive destruction of the Lord's enemies (Revelation 19:14–15).

Joshua assigned portions of the Promised Land to the tribes (Joshua 11:18; 13:1). **Jesus** will give His people their promised inheritance (1 Peter 1:3–5; 2 Peter 3:13).

Joshua led the Israelites to a place of rest (Joshua 21:44). **Jesus** leads us into our spiritual rest (Hebrews 4:8–9).

The Lord had promised Joshua that He would be with him just as He had been with Moses. Joshua wisely waited upon the Lord for his marching orders and became one of those people in the Old Testament who met the pre-incarnate Christ (Joshua 5:13–15):

Now when Joshua was near Jericho, he looked up and saw a man standing in front of him with a drawn sword in his hand. Joshua went up to him and asked, "Are you for us or for our enemies?"

"Neither," he replied, "but as commander of the army of the LORD *I have now come." Then Joshua fell facedown to the ground in reverence, and asked him, "What message does my Lord have for his servant?"*

The commander of the LORD's army replied, "Take off your sandals, for the place where you are standing is holy." And Joshua did so.

Recognizing that this Captain of the armies of God was not merely a man, but God Himself, Joshua fell at His feet to worship. Christ reminded him that He was the Commander. Despite the heavy burden of leadership Joshua was feeling, he was not the true leader; he was only second in command. Stuart Briscoe put His appearance this way: The Lord didn't come to take sides; He came to take over.

The Lord told him, as He had told Moses beside a burning bush (Exodus 3:5), that he was standing on holy ground. Because God was with him, even heathen territory was "holy ground."

All Joshua had to do was follow the Lord's battle plan and the victory would be his. C. I. Scofield wrote, "We often pray for God to assist us in our plans when we should ask Him to take over and lead us in His plans." When Joshua followed God's plans, the Lord blessed him with overwhelming victories. Immense city walls even fell flat at the sound of a shout (Joshua 6)!

Judging Israel

Even though Joshua was Moses' successor, the Lord didn't appoint a national leader for Israel after Joshua died. There was a reason for this: they were not now living in one large group, as they had in the wilderness, but in their own sections of the land. More importantly, they were to be a true theocracy with the Lord as their national leader. The people had stayed somewhat faithful during the lifetime of Joshua but, after he and the elders who had followed him died, chaos erupted. It was the Dark Ages of Israel.

The Roman philosopher Cicero (born 106 BC) said of his day: "Times are bad. Children no longer obey their parents, and everyone is writing a book." Many would say that describes America today, but these things were especially true of Israel in the time of the judges. (Except for the "everyone is writing a book" part.) But someone—possibly Samuel—did write a book about it. The Book of Judges was meant to help future Israelites not repeat that disreputable part of their past.

We see in the Book of Judges partial victories, compromise, and flat-out disobedience. Historically, this period covers about 350 years from the death of Joshua to the anointing of Saul as king. It begins in compromise and ends in anarchy and contains seven apostasies, seven servitudes, and seven deliverances. Since seven usually symbolizes completion in the Bible, we could say that the period of the judges was *complete*—a complete mess.

The beginning of the book is a synopsis of the whole as it tells us that, rather than killing or driving out all the inhabitants of the land, many of the tribes fought for a while and then gave up. They may not have had a "coexist" bumper sticker on their ox carts, but they certainly tried coexisting with the natives of the land. After all, some among them probably urged, it was more enlightened than fighting. Despite God's promise that He had given them all the Promised Land—if they would fight for it they would have victory—*not one tribe* was able to possess all its territory. The tribe of Dan was even chased into the mountains by the local enemies that they failed to dislodge (1:35). I wonder if they ever said to each other, "Oh, that's why the Lord said to drive them out!"

A vicious cycle took hold in which the Israelites in a localized area were harassed and sometimes enslaved by the pagan people around them. What happened was exactly what God had said would happen (Numbers 33:55–56). Then the people cried out to God and, graciously, He raised up a judge to help them. There were 13 judges mentioned in the book (13 is symbolic for the number of rebellion or apostasy). None of these judges were national leaders, but men and one woman each in their own local areas. The people were delivered because of the judge's action but soon went back to their evil ways. Consequently, the Lord allowed them to get into dire straits until they cried out to Him again. And it was déjà vu all over again. And again. And again.

Someone has said, "Extraordinary times call for extraordinary measures." Things became so bad in Israel that the angel of the Lord—the pre-incarnate Christ—appeared to tell them that their disobedience was causing their defeats. Notice the first-person rhetoric that shows this was not just an angel, but God speaking (Judges 2:1–7):

The angel of the LORD went up from Gilgal to Bokim and said, "I brought you up out of Egypt and led you into the land I swore to give to your ancestors. I said, 'I will never break my covenant with you, and you shall not make a covenant with the people of this land, but you shall break down their altars.' Yet you have disobeyed me. Why have you done this? And I have also said, 'I will not drive them out before you; they will become traps for you, and their gods will become snares to you.'"

When the angel of the LORD had spoken these things to all the Israelites, the people wept aloud, and they called that place Bokim. There they offered sacrifices to the LORD.

Maybe the children of Israel had somehow expected the Lord to miraculously drive out the inhabitants of the land for them. He had warned them that wasn't going to happen and that the people they allowed to stay would be a constant problem, ensnaring them with their idols.

The people wept (*Bokim* means "weeping") and offered sacrifices, but it was much too little, much too late. It also didn't represent real repentance. The Book of Judges recorded a time when "every man did what was right in his own eyes" (1:1; 20:18)—a period of virtual lawlessness.

And yet . . . God did not abandon them. He raised up judges to deliver them from their enemies. Some believe that the judges were each a type of Christ in their function as statesman-savior for their people. That may be true in a broad sense, but the judges had flaws or handicaps that made it difficult for them to act. And we know that Jesus had no flaws. In Deborah's case (Judges 4), just being a woman in that culture was a handicap to leadership. Nevertheless, the judges did what they needed to do, although often with complaining, fear, distrust, and/or disobedience. (In that regard, the judges seem to be more types of us than types of Christ.)

Because it was such an evil period, the Lord doesn't directly appear much in the book, but He did appear to the parents of the thirteenth judge, Samson. The pre-incarnate Christ appeared as "the angel of the Lord" to Manoah's wife in Judges 13 and foretold that she would have a son. He instructed her to raise him as a Nazirite which means "devoted." The vows given in Numbers 6:2–6 said that the Nazirite was to abstain from alcohol (and even grapes), to avoid touching anything dead, and was not to cut his hair. This was meant to show others that the person was totally dedicated to the things of the Lord.

When Manoah's wife told her husband about the "man of God," he prayed for a return visit. (We don't know if this reflected a distrust of his wife's word or just a desire to hear this man for himself.) God answered his prayer. Manoah wanted to feed the "man of God" a meal. He refused but said they could make a burnt offering to the Lord. Manoah asked His name, but the divine messenger replied, it is "beyond understanding" (v. 18). In the KJV this is translated "secret" and it is the same Hebrew word in Isaiah 9:6 that tells us the Savior's name is "wonderful." If the couple hadn't figured it out yet, the divine figure suddenly ascended back to heaven in the flame of the offering.

Once Manoah and his wife realized they had spoken with God, Manoah knew they would die (13:19–23). But his wife was more practical (as women often are). She pointed out that God had brought fire to their sacrifice—meaning He accepted it. And God's promise of a son to be born to them obviously couldn't be kept if they died.

When their son was born, they gave him the name Samson, which meant "sunny." No little boy ever had a better start and a chance to do great things for God. After he was grown, the Holy Spirit came upon him numerous times and gave him supernatural strength to defeat the enemies of his people. But God's presence with him depended on Samson keeping his Nazirite vow. And Samson didn't. He broke his vow in every way and ultimately gave away the secret of his strength to Delilah. "Sunny" ended up in the dark. Joseph Parker said that Samson was "an elephant in strength [but] a babe in weakness."

Samson was captured and bound by the Philistines, blinded, and made to turn a millstone to grind grain. Normally the job of an ox. As someone has said, Samson is an illustration that "sin binds and sin blinds and sin grinds." The thirteenth judge didn't live for God but, after he repented, he willingly died for Him. He brought the Philistine temple down on himself with about 3,000 of Israel's enemies in it (16:26–30), killing more in his death than he had in life.

How different from Samson was Jesus who had the strength to escape the cross but didn't. Jesus allowed Himself to be killed, not to take His enemies with Him, but to offer them the forgiveness that could eternally save them.

Boaz and Christ, Kinsman-Redeemers
The events in the Book of Ruth also happened during the period of the judges. Naomi and her family went to the pagan land of Moab trying to escape the famine in Israel (Ruth 1). It was not an act of faith, but of desperation. While there, Naomi's husband and both sons died. Having lost the men she loved and having no means of support, Naomi decided to return to Bethlehem. Her Moabitess daughter-in-law, Ruth, pledged to go with her and be her family until death parted them.

They arrived in Bethlehem at harvest time. Although depressed, Naomi remembered the Law well enough to know the poor could gather what the reapers left. According to Leviticus 19:9–10, that amount was not to be scraps left after repeated reaping, but what remained after only one reaping, as well as anything accidentally dropped. This could amount to 30% of the harvest!

Naomi asked Ruth to go and glean in the fields. It was a "food stamp" program for the poor of that day, but people had to do the work involved in getting it. Ruth showed love for her mother-in-law and an exceptionally good spirit as she did the work of a field hand to support them. As Norman Geisler wrote, Ruth was a "lily in the mud pond of Judges."

There are no coincidences with God; the fact that Ruth "happened" to wind up in fields belonging to Boaz was part of God's plan. Boaz was more than kind to her; he fell in love with her. And after she asked him to (3:1–9), he set out to redeem her future by becoming her (Hebrew) *goel*—kinsman-redeemer.

Boaz is a type of Christ. To be a kinsman-redeemer, Boaz had to have the right, will, and power to redeem. He had to be a near relative of the deceased and able to marry the widow and raise children in his name. There was a relative closer who wanted to redeem the property but didn't want to mess up his estate with another marriage. In her poverty, Naomi probably had no property at this time but, in the year of Jubilee, her husband's property would return to their family who originally owned it. Possibly, that time was near.

After the other relative relinquished his redemption right, Boaz gladly became the kinsman-redeemer and married Ruth. Not coincidentally, because of his heritage, Boaz had no problem marrying a Moabitess. One of his ancestors was Rahab the harlot, who had helped the spies before the siege of Jericho and had been accepted as a proselyte into Judaism (Joshua 6:25). The son born to Ruth and Boaz became the grandfather of King David and an ancestor of Jesus.

The similarities are clear: Christ is our Kinsman-Redeemer. Born as a human baby (also in Bethlehem), He had *the right* as our kinsman to redeem us. He was *willing* to redeem us and was (like Boaz) the only one who truly was. Because He was sinless, He had *the power* to redeem sinful mankind—although He would have to give His life to do it. And for each one who asks Him to be their Kinsman-Redeemer (as Ruth asked of Boaz), He still agrees.

Chapter 13
Making History

In his book *Tell It Slant* about Jesus' words, Eugene Peterson tells about a seminar he led at a seminary which included experienced pastors and priests. The topic one day was Jesus' parables. One of the participants was a Jesuit missionary on sabbatical from 20 years at a post in Africa. When they were discussing parables, Father Tony Byrnne told them about his Africans who loved storytelling and parables. He said that they didn't have enough priests so they tried to recruit lay people to carry out the teaching and deacon work. When he first began, whenever he found especially bright men he'd take them from their village and send them to Rome, Dublin, Boston or New York for training.

After a couple of years they would return to their villages and begin teaching. But the villagers hated them and wouldn't have anything to do with them. They called those who returned from training a "been-to" but pronounced "bean-to." They said "He's *bean-to* London, he's *bean-to* Dublin, he's *bean-to* New York, he's *bean-to* Boston." Why did the people hate them?

Peterson wrote, "They hated the *bean-to* because he no longer told stories. He gave explanations. He taught them doctrines. He gave them directions. He drew diagrams on a chalk board. The *bean-to* left all his stories in the wastebaskets of the libraries and lecture halls of Europe and America. The intimate and dignifying process of telling a parable had been sold for a mess of academic pottage. So, Father Byrnne told us, he quit the practice of sending the men off to those storyless schools."

The power of story is clear in the stories contained in Jewish history. Even though the historical section of the Bible has been called "the pots and pans section," we rarely hear lessons or sermons from it. Nevertheless, with just a few words, almost anyone with a few years of Sunday School under their belt can recall events from the historical books that teach unforgettable lessons:

> David and Goliath
> Saul and the witch of Endor
> Elijah and the prophets of Baal
> A fiery chariot to heaven

The Best Teacher
Georg Wilhelm Friedrich Hegel said, "We learn from history that we do not learn from history." It certainly seems that way because mankind keeps making the same mistakes over and over. World War I was at first called "The Great War" and dubbed the "War to End All Wars." It had to be given a number when Hitler's evil plans to conquer his neighbors and Hirohito's bombing of Pearl Harbor caused another worldwide conflagration.

Even when we're slow to learn from it, history can be an excellent teacher. Maybe that's why God includes in His 39-book Old Testament, 12 books of pure history:

> Joshua
> Judges
> Ruth
> 1 & 2 Samuel
> 1 & 2 Kings
> 1 & 2 Chronicles
> Ezra
> Nehemiah
> Esther

We've already seen that Genesis, Exodus, and Numbers also included the history of the children of Israel. And some of the prophetic books such as Daniel fill in gaps, telling us what was happening while the Jews were in Babylonian captivity.

In the previous chapter, we looked at some of the appearances and types of Christ in the books of Joshua, Judges, and Ruth, the first three books of the historical section of the Bible.

To break down the most basic facts of this part of the history of the Jews:

Pre-1051 BC Israel was a theocracy
First Kingdoms in Israel: Saul 1051 BC; David 1011 BC; Solomon 971 BC
931 BC Kingdom Splits in two under Solomon's son Rehoboam (1 Kings 12):
    Israel = the 10 tribes Northern tribes (King Jeroboam)
    Judah = the 2 tribes Southern tribes (King Rehoboam)
19 Kings in Israel's history—all bad
19 Kings in Judah's history—only 8 good

Although there are appearances of Christ in the historical books, they don't appear as frequently as in the patriarchal period that the Pentateuch covers. Let's look at a few of these appearances and/or types in the historical section.

Samuel, Kings, and Chronicles
If you've ever been confused by how First and Second Chronicles are repetitive of the other historical books at times, Norman Geisler gives a great explanation: First Chronicles covers the same time period as First and Second Samuel. Second Chronicles covers the time period of First and Second Kings. Geisler says, "The history of the kings in Samuel and Kings was written from a prophetic point of view whereas the Chronicles record the history of the Temple from a priestly viewpoint."

First Samuel begins with a childless woman crying out to the Lord for a child. Hannah promised that if the Lord gave her a son, she would give him back to the Lord to serve Him all his days. He did and she did. Samuel, as a small child, came to live in the tabernacle and to be raised by Eli—who everyone knew had already blown childrearing with his own two sons. Hannah had to have a lot of faith in God as she gave up her little boy and only got to see him one time a year when she brought him a larger set of clothes. In Hannah's song of praise (2:10), we have the first mention of the word that is translated *Christ*: "anointed."

According to Josephus, Samuel was not a small child but about 12 years old when the Lord called to him four times as he slept (1 Samuel 3:4, 6, 8, 10). Because he had never heard the Lord's voice, the first three times he thought it was Eli calling him. Even though Eli hadn't heard the Lord's voice in a long time, he realized that it was God speaking to the boy. Eli instructed him how to respond. When Samuel went back to his bed, he heard the Lord call his name twice. The Lord came and stood near Samuel (although we're not told that Samuel saw Him). The boy answered as Eli had told him, "Speak, for your servant is listening" (3:10).

That's where the lesson for children always ends—and for good reason. Samuel received a message of judgment on Eli's house. Eli's two sons had made themselves contemptible as they served in the tabernacle as priests. They had used their positions to enrich themselves and had even slept with the women there. And Eli had done nothing to restrain them. To his credit, Eli insisted that Samuel repeat the message to him and Samuel did so.

First Samuel 3:21 says, "The Lord continued to appear at Shiloh, and there he revealed himself to Samuel through his word. And Samuel's word came to all Israel." Samuel is sometimes called the fourteenth judge, but these verses show that he also was a prophet delivering the Word of God to the people. Although he did "judge" Israel, he was not like the judges in the book by that name.

Under Samuel's leadership, the people woke up to how bad things were and decided to do something about it. Unfortunately, their remedy was to ask for a king so that they could "be like all the nations" (1 Samuel 8:20). It may not seem like a big sin to want to emulate others, but for Israel it was telling. Wanting a king showed they did not want the King they already had—God—to reign over them.

They didn't want to be set apart as God intended them to be; they wanted to fit in. The king they were first given wasn't God's choice but reflected their desires. He looked good. Saul was taller than anyone in the country; he looked kingly. But his heart wasn't God's and his reign—until God took the kingdom from him—was rife with disobedience. God wanted to put on the throne a man "after God's own heart": David.

David, a Royal Learning Curve
While in England, I bought a book that had bios of all the kings and queens in their history. Even though the bios were short, each included both good and bad. Some did great good for their people, such as Queen Victoria who reigned 64 years. Others had short reigns where most of their time was consumed trying to hold onto their power. Some lost their thrones—and their heads.

Power and riches didn't prevent kings and queens from having the problems and pain that is common to all people. We live much more comfortably with our thermostat-controlled homes than kings and queens of vast empires before the 20th century. If you've ever walked through one of their drafty castles on a cold day, you know what I mean. Today we have fewer diseases (or more treatments) and generally live longer than most powerful magistrates of the past. I think often of Queen Anne of England who had 17 children; all of them died in infancy or early childhood. How sad to be able to control much of what happens in an empire and yet have no control over matters closest to your heart!

The Bible tells us the history of King David before and during the 40 years he ruled over Israel. It also tells us the good and bad of this monarch's life. David had some serious sins that God allowed us to know about. In a fill-in-the-blank questionnaire, if we saw "David and _____," some of us might put <u>Goliath</u> in the blank. But many would put <u>Bathsheba</u>. David's most infamous sins, adultery with Bathsheba and killing her husband, Uriah, damaged his reputation with his people. Neither have they been forgotten through the ages. As Shakespeare said, the wrong men do lives on after them, the good is often buried with their bones.

Yet David is also remembered for the good he did and for the worshipful psalms he wrote. He was a man who loved God deeply and repented of his sins fully (see Psalm 51). He is a testament to the restorative grace of God and is also a type of Christ in many ways:

*David, like Jesus, was born in Bethlehem (1 Samuel 16:4; Matthew 2:1).

*David was a shepherd while Jesus, although not literally a shepherd, called Himself the "Good Shepherd" (1 Samuel 16:11; John 10:11).

*Neither David nor Jesus was considered great by his own family members. David was an unexpected choice for king. He was left in the field with the sheep when Jesse's other sons were gathered so that Samuel could anoint one of them king. Samuel naturally gravitated toward the most handsome brother, but God told him that the Lord doesn't look on the outward appearance but on the heart. After looking over all seven brothers, Samuel asked if that was all the sons Jesse had. Jesse seemed to remember he had one more and sent for his youngest son, David. Likewise, Jesus' meek attitude might have kept Him from being anyone's natural choice for a Warrior-King (1 Samuel 16:7–11; Matthew 13:55–56).

*David's father sent him to his brothers; God the Father sent Jesus to His brethren (1 Samuel 17:17; John 8:42).

*David's brothers rejected and mocked him. Most of the Jews (Jesus' brethren) rejected Him and some mocked Him while He was on the cross (1 Samuel 17:28; John 1:11; Matthew 27:12, 41–42).

*David faced Goliath (a type of Satan) alone in the strength of God. Alistair Begg said that while the Israelite army trembled at the sight of Goliath and saw him as unbeatable, David saw him as uncircumcised and totally without the presence and power and promises of God. The Israelites said he's so big we can't fight him, but David said he's so big I can't miss him. Alone Jesus faced His enemy Satan—who has caused many to tremble—and defeated Him on the cross (1 Samuel 17:50–51; John 16:32).

*David destroyed Goliath and freed the Israelites from being enslaved to the Philistines. While we are more often like the Israelite army trembling in their tents, our champion Jesus destroyed the power of sin and freed us from our lifelong fear of death (1 Samuel 17:9, 52; Hebrews 2:14–15).

*David was anointed king but there was a delay before he was crowned because Saul—even though he was told God had taken the throne from him—didn't give it up. God had to *take* the throne from Saul in order for David to reign. Jesus is our anointed King, but there is a delay in Him taking the throne. One day God will take the throne from Satan, the usurper—called the Prince of this world—and then Jesus will reign literally over earth (Hebrews 1:8–9).

*David was a victorious king who fought enemies besides Goliath. The Lord gave him many victories, and the kingdom was expanded greatly (although still not to the boundaries God had set). Jesus is our Warrior-King who has defeated the most important enemies: Satan and death. Paul wrote that "we are more than conquerors through him who loved us" (Romans 8:37).

The Jesus Elijah Knew

When we think of prophets, we often think of the men who wrote the prophetic books included in the Bible. But there were other great prophets who did no writing that we know of. One of the greatest was Elijah. It is not recorded that the pre-incarnate Christ ever appeared to Elijah in the Old Testament, although He certainly empowered him to do great miracles. We meet Elijah first in 1 Kings

17 when he is sent to tell King Ahab that because of his evil there will be no rain in the land until God sends word through him. Shortly after that, Elijah raised a widow's little boy from the dead and had a fiery victory over 450 prophets of Baal.

We know that Elijah knew (and knows) Jesus because of the story of the Transfiguration in Matthew 17:1–3:

After six days Jesus took with him Peter, James and John the brother of James, and led them up a high mountain by themselves. There he was transfigured before them. His face shone like the sun, and his clothes became as white as the light. Just then there appeared before them Moses and Elijah, talking with Jesus.

Elijah was one of the most revered prophets in Israel's history. To see him standing with Moses on the top of a mountain speaking to Jesus confirmed what the disciples had come to believe: Jesus was their Messiah.

There and Back Again

J.R.R Tolkien's alternate title for his fantasy novel, *The Hobbit*, was *There and Back Again*. That could also be a title for a history of the Jews. The Old Testament historical books tell us they made it to the Promised Land but were later removed from it because of their disobedience—only to return to it later. At least some of them returned.

The books of Ezra and Nehemiah tell the story of the relatively small remnant of Judah who returned after 70 years in captivity. When Nehemiah ends, there is only about 400 years until Jesus is born. These are often called the "silent years" because God did not communicate with the people directly during that time.

The Northern tribes, after their captivity and exile, became scattered and assimilated into other cultures. For all practical purposes, they never came back to their homeland. Their captors brought in people from other lands and placed them in northern

Israel. The few poor people who were left in that part of the land ignored Jewish law and intermarried with the newcomers, producing the Samaritan "half-breeds" that the Jews in Jesus' day so despised.

While some members of Judah (the Southern tribes) returned home when given the opportunity, far more stayed in the places they had grown accustomed to in the Babylonian, and then the Persian, Empire. (Timewise, you can insert the Book of Esther between chapters 6 and 7 of the Book of Ezra.) Nehemiah and Ezra complete the story by showing how the Persian king, Cyrus, allowed Jews who wanted to return to Israel to do so. A later Persian king allowed his cupbearer, Nehemiah, to go to Jerusalem to oversee rebuilding the city wall.

After the historical section, the Bible contains wisdom literature (Job, Psalms, Proverbs, Ecclesiastes, and Song of Solomon) and all the prophetic books, but you could say the time-clock is set at about 11:30 p.m. on their B.C. history as Nehemiah ends. The new day will begin for them when a special Baby is born in Bethlehem. And His birth will become the dividing line for all human history.

Chapter 14
The Jesus David Knew

We began this book looking at Jesus walking with two people on the Emmaus road and explaining to them that all the Old Testament Scriptures spoke of Him. Later that same (first) Easter day, the two from the Emmaus Road found the disciples and began telling them about their experience with the risen Jesus. While they were discussing Him, suddenly He appeared in the room with them. The whole group was frightened, thinking He was a ghost. To reassure them, He showed them His hands and feet. They were filled with joy and wonder but also still had some doubts. So He ate a piece of fish to show them He was real. Then He said,

"When I was with you before, I told you that everything written about me in the law of Moses and the prophets and in the Psalms must be fulfilled." Then he opened their minds to understand the Scriptures (Luke 24:44–45 NLT).

This time Jesus specifically mentioned the Psalms. The Jews had used the Psalms as their hymnal for centuries. But they may not have realized that, just as in their books of prophecy, there were verses in the psalms that spoke of the Messiah, verses that would one day be literally fulfilled. These spoke of the Messiah's life, ministry, death, resurrection, and coming again.

Not Hid from Our Eyes
Did you ever have a line from a song get stuck in your head? For a time when I was thinking about a title for this book, the phrase "hid from our eyes" was doing an endless loop in my brain. It came from a line in the first stanza of an old hymn, "Immortal, Invisible, God Only Wise" (hymn lyrics by Walter C. Smith, 1876):

*1 Immortal, invisible, God only wise,
in light inaccessible **hid from our eyes**,
most blessed, most glorious, the Ancient of Days,
almighty, victorious, thy great name we praise.*

*2 Unresting, unhasting, and silent as light,
nor wanting, nor wasting, thou rulest in might;
thy justice like mountains high soaring above
thy clouds which are fountains of goodness and love.*

*3 To all life thou givest, to both great and small;
in all life thou livest, the true life of all;
we blossom and flourish as leaves on the tree,
and wither and perish; but naught changeth thee.*

*4 Great Father of glory, pure Father of light,
thine angels adore thee, all veiling their sight;
all laud we would render: O help us to see
'tis only the splendour of light hideth thee.*

In another version (the original?) before the 4th and 5th verses were shortened and combined, there was a 5th verse that went like this:

*All laud we would render; O help us to see
'Tis only the splendor of light hideth Thee,
And so let Thy glory, Almighty, impart,
Through Christ in His story, Thy Christ to the heart.*

    I decided against "Hid from Our Eyes" for a title because it became overwhelmingly clear that Jesus isn't hidden from our eyes. The opposite is true. Jesus showed up in so many places in the Old Testament before His womb-entry on Earth that it's hard to miss Him. Yet, millions manage. So I have to believe, like the hymn writer, that it's only the splendor of light that hides Him. And it only hides Him from those who don't want to see. The psalmist David wanted to see.

The Jesus David Sang About

The psalms were the hymnbook of the Jewish people and of the church for centuries. David was called the "sweet psalmist of Israel" (2 Samuel 23:1 NKJV). He wrote at least 73 psalms recorded in the Bible. Like most songwriters, he probably wrote far more than just the ones that were "published."

Some psalms, written by David—and others—predicted specific things about Jesus' life and ministry. Psalm 45 (vv. 6, 8) became the basis for a famous old hymn, "Out of the Ivory Palaces": *Your throne, O God, will last for ever and ever; a scepter of justice will be the scepter of your kingdom. You love righteousness and hate wickedness; therefore God, your God, has set you above your companions by anointing you with the oil of joy. All your robes are fragrant with myrrh and aloes and cassia; from* palaces *adorned with ivory the music of the strings makes you glad.*

In **Psalm 41:9** His betrayal was prophesied: *Even my close friend, someone I trusted, one who shared my bread, has turned against me.* Jesus quoted this in the Upper Room because He knew who would betray Him. A little later, Judas left to collect 30 pieces of silver from the Jewish rulers (John 13:18, 26–30).

Psalm 69:8–9 predicted Jesus wouldn't be understood by His own family: *I am a foreigner to my own family, a stranger to my own mother's children; for zeal for your house consumes me, and the insults of those who insult you fall on me.*

Psalm 146:7b–8 says, *The LORD sets prisoners free, the LORD gives sight to the blind, the LORD lifts up those who are bowed down, the LORD loves the righteous.* We see that Scripture fulfilled repeatedly in the healing ministry of Jesus.

Some psalms talk about the present "reign" of the Lord in our fallen world in a spiritual way, in a "the kingdom is within you" sense:

Psalm 9:7–8 *The LORD reigns forever; he has established his throne for judgment. He rules the world in righteousness and judges the peoples with equity.*

Psalm 11:4 *The LORD is in his holy temple; the LORD is on his heavenly throne. He observes everyone on earth; his eyes examine them.*

Other psalms are about the future reign of Christ in the millennial kingdom on earth:

Psalm 2:6–7 *I have installed my king on Zion, my holy mountain. I will proclaim the LORD'S decree: He said to me, "You are my son; today I have become your father."*

Psalm 24:7–9 *Lift up your heads, you gates; be lifted up, you ancient doors, that the King of glory may come in. Who is this King of glory? The LORD strong and mighty, the LORD mighty in battle. Lift up your heads, you gates; lift them up, you ancient doors, that the King of glory may come in.*

One of the most remarkable things about the psalms is that we often see in them a prophecy that was fulfilled in the cross—where we understand that Jesus did not control what happened (even though He could have).

Psalm 22 predicted how Christ would suffer. Jesus quoted from it while He was on the cross, *"My God, my God why have you forsaken me?"* (v. 1). The psalm describes in detail a crucifixion, even though there was no such thing when David wrote it.

Notice verses 7–8: *All who see me mock me; they hurl insults, shaking their heads. "He trusts in the LORD," they say, "let the LORD rescue him. Let him deliver him, since he delights in him."*

Verses 14–18 described the physical sensation of being hung on a cross: *I am poured out like water, and all my bones are out of joint. My heart has turned to wax; it has melted within me. My mouth is dried up like a potsherd, and my tongue sticks to the roof of my mouth; you lay me in the dust of death.*

The psalm begins in anguish but ends in hope with verse 31 (NLT): *His righteous acts will be told to those not yet born. They will hear about everything he has done.*

Psalm 31:5 Jesus also quoted from this psalm as He died on the cross: *Into your hands I commit my spirit.* But He added "Father" to it. In his commentary on Luke, William Barclay said that Jesus died, it seems, the way a child falls to sleep in his father's arms.

Psalm 34:20 predicted that His bones would not be broken.

Psalm 69:21 was fulfilled when Jesus said from the cross: *They . . . gave me vinegar for my thirst.*

The apostles often used quotations from psalms to explain the mission of Jesus, the Savior the Jews should have been looking for but missed.

Psalm 16 In Acts 2:25–28, Peter used Psalm 16 to explain the divinity and the resurrection (Psalm 16:9–11) of the One the Jews had crucified several months before: *"David said about him: 'I saw the Lord always before me. Because he is at my right hand, I will not be shaken. Therefore my heart is glad and my tongue rejoices; my body also will rest in hope, because you will not abandon me to the realm of the dead, you will not let your holy one see decay. You have made known to me the paths of life; you will fill me with joy in your presence.'"*

Psalm 118:22 says that *"The stone the builders rejected has become the cornerstone."* This image too applies to Christ. Peter explained this to the rulers of Jerusalem (Acts 4:10–11): *then know this, you and all the people of Israel: It is by the name of Jesus Christ of Nazareth, whom you crucified but whom God raised from the dead, that this man stands before you healed.* Jesus is *"the stone you builders rejected, which has become the cornerstone."* (See also 1 Peter 2:7.)

Psalm 110 No psalm David wrote has more of a messianic tone than Psalm 110. It is the psalm most quoted or referred to in the New Testament. Only the Messiah fulfills this description. In the psalm, David brings out three facets of the coming Messiah: He will be a Warrior, an Eternal Priest in the order of Melchizedek (the priest-king mentioned in Genesis 14 and Hebrews 7), and the King who rules every nation. He is David's Lord, but He is also David's Son (descendant).

Jesus tested the Pharisees by asking them about this psalm (Matthew 22:41–46). He asked them how, if the Messiah is David's Son, He could also be David's Lord. They had to admit that the Messiah would be the son of David, and yet Jesus points out that David had ascribed deity to Him. It was an enigma to them how this could be because they expected a very human Messiah-deliverer, maybe like Moses, not a divine one. The point Jesus made caused their mouths to finally shut: "no one dared to ask him any more questions" (v. 46). But, from that day on, they escalated their plans to kill Him.

The House and Lineage of David

After removing Saul, he made David their king. God testified concerning him: 'I have found David son of Jesse, a man after my own heart; he will do everything I want him to do.' "From this man's descendants God has brought to Israel the Savior Jesus, as he promised" (Acts 13:22–23).

King David, this "man after [God's] own heart," wanted to honor the Lord by building a permanent "house" or temple for Him. Even the prophet Nathan thought this sounded like a good idea—until the Lord told him otherwise and sent David a message through him. This message is known as the Davidic Covenant (2 Samuel 7:1–29). In it God reminds David that He had never asked for a permanent house (vv. 5–7). He wanted David to continue shepherding His people, but He gave David credit for having the desire (1 Kings 8:18). David, although probably disappointed, accepted God's decision. He understood that, as someone has said, disappointments can be God's appointments.

God softened the blow with His promise to build David "a house"—a dynasty that would last forever and would culminate in the kingdom rule of the Messiah, Jesus Christ, the Son of David (Luke 1:32–33, 69). It will be seen in His Second Coming when He establishes the promised kingdom. It is "David's throne" that God promises His own Son will occupy.

David's son and the Son of David
Because David was a man of war with a lot of blood on his hands, God told him he wouldn't be allowed to build the temple. His son, Solomon, would build the temple because he was a man of peace. However, it was because David defeated the armies of surrounding countries that Solomon's kingdom had a time of "peace on all sides round about him." David also collected much of the wealth and materials that were used to build the temple.

While we've looked at many types of Christ in the Old Testament, Solomon is a different type. He typifies Christ as the Prince of Peace who will rule over the millennial kingdom, grander than anything yet seen on earth. But, in more personal ways, he's a king who is the opposite of Christ. Jesus said of Himself "something greater than Solomon is here" (Matthew 12:42). A few ways that Christ is far greater:

*Solomon was the wisest man in the world in his time and all nations came to listen to his wisdom (1 Kings 4:34), but Jesus "became to us wisdom from God" (1 Corinthians 1:30).

*Solomon accumulated the greatest wealth any man ever had, but Jesus became poor. Paul wrote, "For you know the grace of our Lord Jesus Christ, that though he was rich, yet for your sake he became poor, so that you by his poverty might become rich" (2

Corinthians 8:9). The riches we are promised are not necessarily material. All believers have been blessed with spiritual riches.

*Solomon built great construction projects by drafting the people into service, but Jesus came to serve, not to be served.

*Solomon's reign was a period where Israel lived in peace with its enemies, but Jesus made it possible for us, who were the enemies of God, to have peace with Him. He made "peace by the blood of his cross" (Colossians 1:20).

*Solomon loved the Lord, but he failed God in many ways with his disobedience. Jesus is the only One who loved the Lord with all His heart and mind and strength and who never failed Him.

*Solomon built a temple that would be torn down (repeatedly), but Jesus is the eternal temple who was raised up. In John 2:19 he said, "Destroy this temple, and in three days I will raise it up." He spoke, not of the temple made of limestone but of His own body. He did this when He rose from the grave.

*Solomon had many wives, but Jesus has one bride—the Church.

Like his father, David, Solomon was a prolific author. He's credited with writing 3,000 proverbs and more than 1,000 songs (1 Kings 4:32.) Many of his proverbs personify wisdom. Go through the Book of Proverbs and substitute "Christ" for "wisdom," and you'll find that the proverb usually still makes sense. Solomon put some proverbs in a collection that makes up most of the Book of Proverbs. He also wrote the Song of Solomon, an allegory about the love of a groom for his bride which beautifully pictures Jesus' love for His bride, the Church.

Solomon may have written his other biblical book, Ecclesiastes, near the end of his life—after he had allowed his many foreign wives and concubines (a total of 1,000 women!) to turn his heart from the Lord (1 Kings 11:1–6). It's a book with a decidedly cynical and humanistic view: "vanity, vanity, all is vanity."

Did Solomon repent and turn back to the Lord at the end of his life? It doesn't sound like he did from what we read in the first 11 chapters of Ecclesiastes. But the last chapter shows that he was wise enough to realize he had wasted much of what God gave him. It's the lament of an old man who wishes he could do it all over in a better way. In Ecclesiastes12, he advised others to stay true to God from their youth because the years will pass by quickly (Ecclesiastes 12:13–14):

> *Now all has been heard;*
> *here is the conclusion of the matter:*
> *Fear God and keep his commandments,*
> *for this is the duty of all mankind.*
> *For God will bring every deed into judgment,*
> *including every hidden thing,*
> *whether it is good or evil.*

If he learned from his mistakes, maybe Solomon was pretty wise after all.

PART III
THE JESUS THE PROPHETS KNEW

Chapter 15
The Suffering Savior Isaiah Knew

What if in March 2001, a man had started walking the streets of New York City wearing a large sign that read, "Beware! Terrorists are going to fly planes into the twin towers and kill 3,000 people." He could have walked for miles every day for almost six months with that message and never gained credibility. He still would have been considered a kook by everyone. People might have walked on the other side of the street to avoid him. They would probably have laughed and said, "That could never happen." But on September 11, 2001 by evening, every major news organization would have been trying to find him. They would want to ask him how he knew what was going to happen—what *had* happened that morning. And they would have all wondered what might have happened if everyone hadn't discounted the messenger.

The Old Testament prophets were a little like that imaginary man with the sign. They lived in communities that, for the most part, did not believe their prophecies—even when they saw their short-term prophecies come true. And they always did. For true prophets, no mistakes were allowed; every single prophecy had to come true. That is the record of each of the 16 prophets whose name is also the name of a book in the Bible. We revere them now, yet they were often the most hated men in town. Why? Because they told the people what God expected of them. And, like people today, the people of that day didn't want to be told they were sinning.

Because I sometimes became confused about the prophets—when they lived and who they prophesied to—I made a little cheat-sheet that I keep in that section of my Bible. Maybe it will help you too. (They are grouped by the people they warned and whether they prophesied before their audience was taken into exile or during or after their period of exile):

Pre-exilic Prophets to Israel (the 10 northern tribes) before 722 BC when Assyria captured Israel (2 Kings 17): Amos and Hosea

Pre-exilic Prophets to Judah (the two southern tribes) before 586 BC when Babylon captured Judah (2 Kings 25): Jeremiah, Isaiah, Micah, Zephaniah, Habakkuk, Joel

Exile Prophets with the Jews in captivity to give them hope: Jeremiah (who also wrote Lamentations), Ezekiel, Daniel

Post-exilic Prophets to encourage Judah which was allowed to return home in Cyrus' reign after Persia conquered Babylon: Haggai, Zechariah, Malachi

Prophets to Other Nations: Obadiah (message to Edom), Jonah & Nahum (messages to Nineveh)

When I've taught from prophetic books, it became obvious that even people who had been in church and reading the Bible all their lives were sometimes confused. Would it surprise you to know that the prophets themselves were confused by the messages God asked them to deliver? Peter spoke of this (1 Peter 1:10–11): "Concerning this salvation, the prophets, who spoke of the grace that was to come to you, searched intently and with the greatest care, trying to find out the time and circumstances to which the Spirit of Christ in them was pointing when he predicted the sufferings of the Messiah and the glories that would follow."

The prophets wondered what was going on when their own messages seemed to paint conflicting pictures of the coming Messiah—here talking about a gentle, suffering Savior and there talking about an all-powerful King taking vengeance on His enemies and ruling absolutely.

Commentators have compared the disparity to looking out at two mountain ranges in the distance. The first is several miles away, while the second is much farther. The heights of the mountains can't be determined by the naked eye. What also can't be seen is a vast valley between the mountain ranges. That valley is where we live now, looking back on the arrival of Jesus more than 2,000 years ago that fulfilled every prophecy about it perfectly. And we can trust that the Second Coming—whenever it happens—will fulfill the many prophecies about it.

When Isaiah Saw the Lord
The prophet Isaiah's 66-chapter book contains many prophecies. Parts of 47 chapters of his book are quoted or alluded to more than 400 times in the New Testament. (Only the Book of Psalms has more mentions.)

Early in his book Isaiah tells us about when he "saw the Lord." This can cause some to balk because we know the Bible says, "no one has ever seen God." And yet, throughout this book we've seen people who heard and sometimes saw God: Adam and Eve, Enoch, Abraham, Jacob, Moses, the 70 elders, Joshua, Samuel . . . The perceived conflict becomes much clearer with Jesus' explanation: "No one has seen the Father except the one who is from God; only he has seen the Father" (John 6:46). Jesus said that no one has seen *God the Father*. Who they saw, both in the Old Testament in a theophany or vision and in the New Testament in the flesh, was God the Son. He came to reveal God to man. But it goes even further than that. In the Upper Room Philip said,

"Lord, show us the Father and that will be enough for us." Jesus answered: "Don't you know me, Philip, even after I have been among you such a long time? Anyone who has seen me has seen the Father. How can you say, 'Show us the Father'? Don't you believe that I am in the Father, and that the Father is in me? The words I say to you I do not speak on my own authority. Rather, it is the Father, living in me, who is doing his work. (John 14:8–10)

Because of Christ's appearances in the earlier parts of the Bible, we certainly shouldn't be surprised when Isaiah says that he saw the Lord. His account begins in Isaiah 6:1, "In the year that king Uzziah died, I saw the Lord high and exalted, seated on a throne; and the train of his robe filled the temple."

Isaiah doesn't satisfy our curiosity because he describes more about the angelic worship going on around God than what God actually looked like. Maybe, like Paul who was taken to the third heaven, he was told not to reveal all that he'd seen. We don't know how old Isaiah was when this happened, but we know that what he saw changed his life and ministry. He got his eyes off what the king had been doing (the king was now dead) and put them on what the coming King would do. Maybe that's why God entrusted Him with so many prophecies.

An Unconventional Arrival
When the movie *The Hiding Place,* Corrie ten Boom's story about how her family helped Jews to escape the Nazis, premiered in 1975, it had gotten almost no media coverage. Billy Graham was at the premiere as well as Corrie ten Boom and the actress who played her, Jeannette Clift George. That might have been the end of it, and it would have become one of those good, but minimally acclaimed Christian films. However, that night someone tried to stop the showing of the film by throwing a bomb marked with a swastika and filled with poison gas into the theater. Everyone had to be evacuated. Fire trucks as well as ambulances arrived to take those made ill by the gas to the hospital. The attendees stood outside the theater for a while hoping that the movie could resume, but Billy Graham announced that for safety reasons, it had to be cancelled.

What a shame! Or was it? The next day coverage of the film was on every news show—morning, noon, and night—and there were headlines in papers around the world about what had happened at the premiere of *The Hiding Place.* Undoubtedly, many people then decided to see this headline news-making movie.

God doesn't need PR people—He has His own ways.

Similarly, when God communicated with the prophets, He didn't always use conventional ways or methods. Sometimes He spoke to prophets, like Daniel, through dreams. Other times He appeared to them in a symbolic vision such as the spinning, glowing wheels in Ezekiel 1. But of all the unconventional ways that God appeared to His people, surely the most unconventional would be Almighty God allowing Himself to become an embryo . . . a fetus . . . a baby. And to be born to a poor young woman and raised in a backwater village of a small Mid-eastern country.

Here are a few prophecies of Jesus' birth and childhood, found in the Old Testament ➔ and their New Testament fulfillments:

I see him, but not now; I behold him, but not near. A star will come out of Jacob; a scepter will rise out of Israel (Numbers 24:17). ➔ *After Jesus was born in Bethlehem in Judea, during the time of King Herod, Magi from the east came to Jerusalem and asked, "Where is the one who has been born king of the Jews? We saw his star when it rose and have come to worship him* (Matthew 2:1).

But you, Bethlehem Ephrathah, though you are small among the clans of Judah, out of you will come for me one who will be ruler over Israel, whose origins are from of old, from ancient times" (Micah 5:2). ➔ *So Joseph also went up from the town of Nazareth in Galilee to Judea, to Bethlehem the town of David, because he belonged to the house and line of David. . . . While they were there, the time came for the baby to be born, and she gave birth to her firstborn, a son. She wrapped him in cloths and placed him in a manger, because there was no guest room available for them* (Luke 2:4–5, 7).

Therefore the Lord himself will give you a sign: The virgin will conceive and give birth to a son, and will call him Immanuel (Isaiah 7:14). ➔ *In the sixth month of Elizabeth's pregnancy, God sent the angel Gabriel to Nazareth, a town in Galilee, to a virgin pledged to be married to a man named Joseph, a descendant of David. The virgin's name was Mary* (Luke 1:26–27).

When Israel was a child, I loved him, and out of Egypt I called my son (Hosea 11:1). ➔ *So [Joseph] got up, took the child and his mother during the night and left for Egypt. And so was fulfilled what the Lord had said through the prophet: "Out of Egypt I called my son"* (Matthew 2:14–15).

A voice is heard in Ramah, mourning and great weeping, Rachel weeping for her children and refusing to be comforted, because they are no more (Jeremiah 31:15). ➔ *When Herod realized that he had been outwitted by the Magi, he was furious, and he gave orders to kill all the boys in Bethlehem and its vicinity who were two years old and under, in accordance with the time he had learned from the Magi. Then what was said through the prophet Jeremiah was fulfilled: "A voice is heard in Ramah, mourning and great weeping, Rachel weeping for her children and refusing to be comforted, because they are no more"* (Matthew 2:16–18).

His Coming Announced

In his book, Zechariah gives more messianic prophecies than any of the other 11 minor prophets and more than all of the prophets, except Isaiah. He experienced a series of eight night visions (all in the same night!). Some had a specific meaning for his time; others had a meaning for the future.

Almost every churchgoer is familiar with the Palm Sunday passage that originates in Zechariah 9. All four gospels tell the story of Jesus entering Jerusalem riding on a donkey colt at the end of His three years of ministry and miracle working. All the gospels except Luke quote Zechariah 9:9. Some have called this Jesus' "triumphal entry," but it only could have been considered "triumphal" if the Jews had accepted Him as their one true King at that time. The kingdom would have come in . . . and you and I probably would have never been born. One commentator said that Jesus did not intend this to be a triumphal entry; instead, it was a tearful entry. Luke 19:41–44 tells us that He wept over Jerusalem and her future fate. He was arranging an exit from the world, not an entrance into the kingdom.

Conquering kings rode horses into cities when they came in war. A donkey was what a king rode when he came in peace. Riding a donkey *colt* would have looked less kingly and even more humble. Possibly Jesus' feet drug the ground. People may have whispered, "Couldn't His disciples have found him a better ride?" Jesus—then and now—often doesn't do things the way we think they should be done.

Most of the people greeting Him saw this as the fulfillment of Zechariah 9, so they hailed Him with palm branches and laid their clothes down like a red carpet. They chanted "Hosanna" which means "Save" or "Save now!" And He would save—a few days later. Only it would be a much different kind of salvation that they expected. To those who shouted that He should control the people, He said that if they hadn't shouted, the rocks on the ground would have cried out.

Zechariah had also prophesied that this One who was coming would remove the sin of the land "in a single day" (3:9). We've come to call that one day, Good Friday.

The Suffering Servant: Isaiah 53
Rather than a verse here and a verse there that refers to Christ, all of Isaiah 53 speaks of Christ: His life and ministry (vv. 1–4), His death (vv. 5–8), burial (v. 9), and exaltation (vv. 10–12). Although Isaiah wrote this about 700 years before the Messiah came, it is a perfect description of much of the life and death of Christ. Isaiah 53 (quoted here in New King James Version) is referred to in the New Testament more than any other Old Testament chapter:

Who has believed our report?
And to whom has the arm of the LORD *been revealed?*
² For He shall grow up before Him as a tender plant,
And as a root out of dry ground.
He has no form or comeliness;
And when we see Him,
There is no beauty that we should desire Him.
³ He is despised and rejected by men,
A Man of sorrows and acquainted with grief.
And we hid, as it were, our faces from Him;
He was despised, and we did not esteem Him.
⁴ Surely He has borne our griefs
And carried our sorrows;
Yet we esteemed Him stricken,
Smitten by God, and afflicted.
⁵ But He was wounded for our transgressions,
He was bruised for our iniquities;
The chastisement for our peace was upon Him,
And by His stripes we are healed.

Most Jewish expositors applied this chapter to the Messiah until the 12th century. Then they began applying it to the nation Israel. But, Israel couldn't die for the sins of Israel (v. 8) so that interpretation doesn't make sense. Maybe because it is so clearly a description of the Messiah—which was fulfilled in Jesus— it is rarely read in the synagogues. It has even been dubbed "the Bad Conscience of the Synagogues." If I were witnessing to a Jew, this is the Old Testament passage I would use.

Isaiah 53:2 says that He was like a young plant, a root out of dry ground. He had come from the line of David (in Isaiah 11:1–3 that Branch was promised) but in an unexpected time and way. It also tells us He probably didn't look like Jim Caviezel, the handsome actor in *The Passion of the Christ* movie. If by any chance the Shroud of Turin has the real imprint of His face, it showed a long, thin face with a Middle Eastern nose or one that had been broken in the beatings He endured. The historian Josephus described Jesus as a tall man with brown hair cut in the chin-length Roman style. There was nothing remarkable in His looks that would stop donkey traffic on the Jericho road. The people looked for a conquering king; they got a suffering Servant.

He was "acquainted with grief" or "familiar with suffering." How did Jesus suffer *before* the Cross? He may have never had a disease; nature didn't seem to attack Him. Unbroken colts let Him ride on their backs, and storms obeyed His commands. But He suffered. He knew extreme hunger from fasting 40 days in the wilderness. He knew the pain of cramped muscles from hard work as a carpenter. He knew the sorrow of losing His earthly adoptive father and the distress of knowing that His half-brothers and sisters didn't believe in Him (until after He was resurrected). They thought He was their poor, crazy brother. He suffered many of the same things regular human beings suffer—only infinitely more so.

Jesus suffered *more* because He had divine knowledge and foreknowledge. John 2:25 tells us He knew what was in man—how weak we are, although we try hard not to be. He knew that Judas would betray Him. He knew that Peter would deny Him—even though he'd sworn he wouldn't. He knew the rest of the disciples would run away. Except for John. (No wonder He gave the care of His mother to steadfast John.)

Jesus knew what horrible suffering He would go through on the Cross. He would bear the physical pain which would have been excruciating for about six hours. But more than that, He would be separated, because of the sin He bore for us, from His Father. In all eternity the Father and Son had never been separated for even a moment. He knew it before He allowed Himself to be born as a baby. He knew it would be necessary to redeem man before the foundation of the world and the creation of human beings. Yet, He created us anyway.

It was *our* griefs and *our* sorrows that He carried. He was wounded for *our* transgressions and iniquities. (vv. 4–5). God reminds us through Isaiah why the Suffering Servant had to suffer. For us. It was our punishment, not His. We are healed by His stripes or His wounds, but the healing is not something we claim as a cure for all our sicknesses. The context talks about our transgressions and iniquities, not our diabetes and cancer. The word for "healed" in Hebrew sometimes refers to healing disease, but it was also used for healing of the soul. As Psalm 41:4 (NKJV) says, "Lord, be merciful to me; Heal my soul, for I have sinned against You." First Peter 2:24 makes it clear this healing by His stripes is for sin: "He himself bore our sins in his body on the tree, so that we might die to sins and live for righteousness; by his wounds you have been healed."

The Shepherd and the Lamb
Isaiah turns his eyes from the suffering of Jesus for just a moment to how those He came to save react:

⁶ All we like sheep have gone astray;
We have turned, every one, to his own way;
And the Lord has laid on Him the iniquity of us all.
⁷ He was oppressed and He was afflicted,
Yet He opened not His mouth;
He was led as a lamb to the slaughter,
And as a sheep before its shearers is silent,
So He opened not His mouth.
⁸ He was taken from prison and from judgment,
And who will declare His generation?
For He was cut off from the land of the living;
For the transgressions of My people He was stricken.
⁹ And they made His grave with the wicked—
But with the rich at His death,
Because He had done no violence,
Nor was any deceit in His mouth.

Isaiah talked about us as wayward sheep (v. 6) and God as the Shepherd but, in verses 7–8, he talks about Jesus as the sacrificial Lamb. (Jesus is called the Lamb 28 times in the book of Revelation.) Jesus didn't resist arrest or let His disciples resist in the Garden of Gethsemane. Nor did He defend Himself in the illegal trials. He was in the role of a servant, and a servant doesn't talk back.

Legal experts who have studied the arrest and trials of Jesus characterize them as a complete miscarriage of justice, but God foreknew and allowed all of it to happen. In the garden Jesus told His disciples that He could have called 10,000 angels to free Him from what was about to happen (Matthew 26:53). Even one angel could have done it; Scripture tells us one angel killed 185,000 men (Isaiah 37:36). But Isaiah's prophecy had to be fulfilled that He would be cut off from the land of the living (v. 8). There would be no remission of sins without the shedding of blood—and the blood that was necessary was His holy blood.

He died with the wicked, surrounded by thieves on crosses—only one of them repentant—and was buried in the borrowed tomb of Joseph of Arimathea (v. 9). Usually the bodies of criminals were thrown on the garbage heap in the Valley of Gehenna to rot or be burned, but Jesus was buried in a rich man's tomb. The Garden Tomb (the Protestant site) that tourists see in Jerusalem is a beautiful garden surrounding a first-century tomb hewn in rock. You bend your head to go into it, look to the side and see the rock shelf that would have held one body. Scientific tests on that bench indicate that a body never decomposed on it. It's such a nice tomb you wonder why—unless it was Jesus' tomb and He didn't decompose at all. Would Joseph have had himself buried in the tomb he'd loaned for a weekend to his resurrected Lord? Most people wouldn't feel worthy.

[10] *Yet it pleased the* LORD *to bruise Him;*
He has put Him to grief.
When You make His soul an offering for sin,

He shall see His seed, He shall prolong His days,
And the pleasure of the LORD *shall prosper in His hand.*
¹¹ He shall see the labor of His soul, and be satisfied.
By His knowledge My righteous Servant shall justify many,
For He shall bear their iniquities.
¹² Therefore I will divide Him a portion with the great,
And He shall divide the spoil with the strong,
Because He poured out His soul unto death,
And He was numbered with the transgressors,
And He bore the sin of many,
And made intercession for the transgressors.

By inspiration, Isaiah began in verse 10*b* to use the future tense, showing a break between the Messiah's suffering and death and His resurrection. The righteous Servant by His sacrifice would justify *many* (v. 11), but it's not a universal salvation. Only those who personally accept His sacrifice are saved. Nevertheless, if everyone who has ever lived plus everyone who is yet to live received Him as their Savior, His "intercession for the transgressors" (v. 12) would still be sufficient.

When you remember that the idea of a Suffering Savior was completely foreign to the Jews' concept of a Messiah, it is all the more remarkable that Isaiah would write this.

And Many More

The Branch of the Lord	Isaiah 4:2
The Teacher	Isaiah 30:19–26
The Foundation Stone	Isaiah 28:16
The Servant of the Lord	Isaiah 42:1–7
Messiah's Gethsemane	Isaiah 50:4–9
Proclaimer of Good News	Isaiah 61:1–3
The Lord Our Righteousness	Jeremiah 23:5–6
The Promise Keeper	Jeremiah 33:14–16
The Tender Sprig	Ezekiel 17:22–24
The Good Shepherd	Ezekiel 34:23–31
The Son of Man	Daniel 7:13–14
Our High Priest	Zechariah 3:8–10
Rejected Good Shepherd	Zechariah 11:4–14
The Pierced One	Zechariah 12:10
The Betrayed One	Zechariah 13:7
Sold for Silver	Zechariah 13:12–13
Messenger of the Covenant	Malachi 3:1

Chapter 16
The Reigning Savior Daniel Knew

Frederick Buechner in *Telling the Truth* wrote this about Shakespeare's later writing:

"At the close of his career, after the period of the great tragedies, Shakespeare turned to something much closer to true fairy tales. He wrote *Cymbeline*, where innocence is vindicated and old enemies reconciled, and *The Winter's Tale*, where the dead queen turns out not to be dead at all, the lost child, Perdita, restored to those who love her. And he wrote *The Tempest* itself, where the same great storm of the world that drowned the Franciscan nuns aboard the *Deutschland* and lashed old Lear to madness and stung Job in his despair is stilled by Prospero's magic; and justice is done, and lovers reunited, and the kingdom restored to its rightful king so that in a way it is the beautiful dream of Caliban that turns out to be real and the storm of the world with all its cloud-capped towers and gorgeous palaces and solemn temples that turns out to be the insubstantial pageant that fades into thin air and leaves not a rack behind."

You don't have to have read everything Shakespeare wrote to see Buechner's point. He noticed that Shakespeare's writing changed as he grew older. With all the stories that ran through his brilliant mind, he wanted to believe that in the end—in real life—things would turn out better and the kingdom would be "restored to its rightful king."

All Shakespeare's writing shows a knowledge of the Bible, and history records that he was a conforming member of the Anglican church. But no one knows if he had a personal faith that involved more than just his name on a church roll. His later works show that he, like many believers through the ages, hoped that one day all things would be put right. It is not an unfounded hope. It is, in fact, what God promised through the prophets will happen.

What Happens Next?
We go back to some of the oldest books in the world to find out what is yet to happen. Here are some interesting facts about the amount of prophecy they contain:

*One-fourth of the books in the Bible are of a prophetic nature.
*One-fifth of the verses throughout the Bible were prophetic at the time written.
*In the Old Testament, 16 of the last 17 books are prophecy.
*In the New Testament, every book of the 27, except 4 (Galatians, Philemon, 2 John and 3 John), has some teaching on the Second Coming.

Prophecies differ, but there is a universal theme. From the time of the prophets, starting almost 3000 years ago, biblical prophecy has said that things will *not* get better in the world, they will get worse until Jesus returns. That can be encouraging as we notice that the world continues to grow worse. As somebody quipped: if I saw a huge pile of manure, I wouldn't despair about how to clean it up. I'd figure there had to be a pony in there somewhere.

An optimist can be defined as someone who is always thinking things will get better while a pessimist thinks things are bad now but, just wait, they're sure to get worse. In *Beyond Doubt*, Cornelius Plantinga Jr. coined an alternate word: "hopetimist." A "hopetimist" says things may not get better, but God is still with us. This life is not all there is. In that regard, the Bible is the ultimate *hopetimistic* book.

Our hope—our assurance—is that even though things continue to get worse, they will culminate in the Second Coming of Christ. And that hope first showed up in the Old Testament.

There are **three major divisions** of prophecy based on what you believe about Christ's kingdom, which the Bible says will last a millennium (1000 years). There also some divisions within those positions:

A-millennial— ("a" means "without") Those who hold this view don't believe in a literal 1,000-year kingdom on earth. They say that it all refers in a general way to faith. However, to believe this, they have to ignore a lot of verses from the Old and New Testaments.

Post-millennial—Early in the 20th century, many held the post-millennial position: people would be so effective at spreading the gospel—and the gospel so irresistible—that they would bring in a spiritual kingdom. After that, Christ returns and the eternal ages begins. They had a saying: "Every day in every way, the world is getting better and better." Then came World War I, the Depression, World War II, the threat of nuclear war, terrorism, etc. Although there still are people who hold this decidedly optimistic post-millennial belief, you can see how it became a less popular theory.

Pre-millennial–This is the view that Christ comes back before the 1000-year reign and, being the only One who can, sets up and reigns over the kingdom. Because a-millennialism is more an *unbelief* than a belief and the prerequisites of post-millennialism seem unlikely, pre-millennialism (to me) makes the most sense. Among pre-millennials there are several differing views concerning the Rapture (1 Thessalonians 4:14–18), the belief that Jesus will take all true believers off the earth before the kingdom begins. The Old Testament forerunner of the idea of the Rapture was Enoch who was translated or taken to heaven without dying. Genesis 5:24 says, "Enoch walked with God; then he was no more, because God took him away."

  ***Pre-Tribulation View:** This is the most popular view for those who believe in the Rapture. (It is the one I hold.) It says Christ comes to the air and takes all living Christians out of the world in order to keep the Church from going through the seven-year

Tribulation period when the wrath of God is poured out on the earth (Revelation 3:10).

***Partial Rapture View:** A view that isn't about the "when" but the "who." It says Christ will rapture believers—but—He will only take those who are actively looking for Him. Hebrews 9:28 is quoted. It's not a widespread view and is supported more by a belief in "works" (earning the right to be raptured) than by Scripture.

***Mid-Tribulation Rapture View:** This says that Christ will take all believers out at the mid-point (3 and 1/2 years) of the seven-year Tribulation, when the "Great Tribulation" starts. Some believe that would coincide with the time the two witnesses in Revelation 11 are raised and visibly ascend, after being killed by the Antichrist. This view has gained some ground recently, possibly because it seems to explain why the world has become far worse than most believers imagined it would before the Rapture takes place.

***Post-Tribulation Rapture View:** It says that Christ will come at the end of the Tribulation and take the Church up as He comes to earth in the visible Second Coming. However, this seems confusing or at least redundant because Scripture says that is the same time He's bringing the Church in heaven down with Him to set up the kingdom (Revelation 19:11–16).

What Daniel Saw

The books of prophecy are called Major or Minor—not to denote importance but to indicate the length of the books. The Book of Daniel, although only 12 chapters long is considered one of the four "Major Prophets," even though the other three prophets (Isaiah, Jeremiah, and Ezekiel) wrote much longer books.

Dr. J. Vernon McGee said, "If Isaiah is the prince of prophets, then Daniel is the king of prophets." Sir Isaac Newton said, "To reject Daniel is to reject the Christian religion." But the greatest authority was Jesus. In His Olivet Discourse, (found in Matthew 24–25, Mark 13, and Luke 21) which talked about prophecy, Jesus quoted from only one Old Testament book: Daniel. In a book by book study of the Bible, it becomes clear that if you want to understand the New Testament prophecy of Revelation, you must understand Daniel.

Daniel records the captivity and religious persecution of the Jews in the first half of his book. His three friends were put in the fiery furnace (chapter 3) for refusing to worship an image of the king. Daniel was thrown into the lions' den (chapter 6) for continuing to worship Jehovah. Christ (the Son of Man) appeared as the fourth man in the fiery furnace and protected His people. And God sent an angel into the lions' den with Daniel. The hungry lions suddenly became as tame as pussycats.

Maybe because Daniel lived so faithfully before his Babylonian captors, God allowed him to see into the future what is happening in heaven. In Daniel 7:9–10, thrones are set in place (notice thrones is *plural*) and the "Ancient of Days" takes His place. (This seems to parallel chapters 4 and 5 in Revelation where John is shown heaven.) It is all described symbolically: white for holiness and purity, a river of fire symbolizing His judgment, flaming wheels (as in Ezekiel 1) speaking of the sovereignty of God and the fact He is constantly at work. It's also similar to the description of Jesus in Revelation 1:12–20, a description of deity. We know the Ancient of Days is God the Father because God the Son is shown being escorted in (Daniel 7:13–14). In the courtroom, books are opened (v. 10). It's clear that God is still in charge and is getting ready to execute judgment.

Daniel gives us a preview of the earthly throne of the Son of God, "He was given authority, glory and sovereign power; all peoples, nations, and men of every language worshipped him. His dominion is an everlasting dominion that will not pass away, and his kingdom is one that will never be destroyed" (7:14).

Here Christ is presented before the throne of the Father and given the everlasting dominion over the nations that He was promised. This is obviously still future. It happens in Revelation 20:1–8 where we are also told six times that His kingdom will last for a thousand years. During that time, kingdom promises made in the Old Testament will be fulfilled. Nature will be delivered from its bondage: the lamb and the wolf will lie down together, the little child can play with snakes. There will be world peace. (Every Miss America contestant who answered a pageant question saying that is what she wanted should be happy about that!)

This vision must have given Daniel great comfort. God allowed him to see that, although his people were captives away from their homeland, one day all these prophecies would be fulfilled. Their Messiah would come and reign on the throne of David. He could look forward with that hope, even though he must have realized that he would not live to see it.

Daniel had many things revealed to him, but it was not for him to know everything. He ended his book with what God told him: "As for you, go your way till the end. You will rest and then at the end of the days you will rise to receive your allotted inheritance" (12:13). Many believe that Old Testament believers will inherit the earthly kingdom, which after the 1000-year period becomes part of the eternal ages. In Revelation 21, the New Jerusalem that comes down out of heaven seems to be suspended over the earth. Maybe that will be the home of the New Testament saints while the New Earth that God creates (a new heaven and a new earth are promised in Revelation 21:1-2) will be the home of redeemed Israel. We're not given every detail of who will live where but, no matter where he is located, Daniel will receive his reward.

Zechariah's Coming King

Prophetic sections are often so intertwined that it can take discernment to separate references to Christ's first coming from His second. In some verses, the two comings are separated by a verse, such as between Isaiah 9:6 and 7. Or even after a comma, such as in Isaiah 61:2. On the first Palm Sunday, which we looked at in the previous chapter, the people saw the fulfillment of their king coming in gentleness and humility riding on a donkey colt, prophesied in

Zechariah 9:9. Chronologically, the whole Church Age fits between verse 9 and verse 10. But, after verse 9, Zechariah begins to write about what will happen at the Second Coming when Jesus returns to defeat His enemies and establish His kingdom. He won't be on a donkey colt. Revelation 19 shows that He'll be riding a white horse and leading the armies of heaven to put down the Battle of Armageddon with a word from His mouth.

When Jesus Christ comes again, Zechariah 9:10 says that "He will proclaim peace to the nations. His rule will extend from sea to sea and from the River to the ends of the earth." Restored to their land and ruled over by their Messiah, the Jews will then "sparkle in his land like jewels in a crown" (v. 16).

From Zechariah 9 through chapter 14 is one of the most concentrated sections of messianic truth in the Bible. In it Christ is shown as Shepherd, Warrior, Deliverer, and the One coming again to reign as the final King "over the whole earth" (Zechariah 14:9).

Malachi: The Sun Also Rises
Did you ever see the movie *Back to the Future* where a teenage boy meets a mad scientist who has rigged a sports car to time travel into the past? Michael J. Fox's teenaged character figures that if he could just get back to where things went wrong with his parents—who drink too much and fight all the time—he could change things. In the movie he goes back in time (and learns a little more about his parents' youth than most of us would want to know). But, amazingly, his plan works: he changes enough in the past so that when he returns to his own time in the future, he finds his family is well-adjusted and happy.

The Bible is a book from the past about the future. Malachi, the last prophecy in the Old Testament, in the middle of his book (3:2–5) switches, not just to 400 years in the future from his day to the first coming of Christ, but to the still-future second coming.

Verse 2–3*a* says, "But who can endure the day of his coming? Who can stand when he appears? For he will be like a refiner's fire or a launderer's soap. He will sit as a refiner and purifier of silver; he will purify the Levites and refine them like gold and silver." If this sounds familiar, it's because there are two sections of Handel's "Messiah" that repeat it. Near the beginning, the sixth and seventh sections are titled "But Who May Abide the Day of His Coming?" and "And He Shall Purify the Sons of Levi." They come straight out of this section. Malachi tells us that one day those who refuse to follow God will realize death didn't end it for them; there is a judgment to come and a second death (which is judgment but not cessation of being).

Malachi wrote, "But to you who fear My name the Sun of Righteousness shall arise with healing in His wings; and you shall go out and grow fat like stall-fed calves" (4:2). When Jesus rises with healing in His wings, He will reign as King of kings. His people will be overcome with joy, like calves let out of small stalls to frolic in a spring meadow. And His victory over evil will be complete.

As he closes, Malachi reminds the people of two faithful men, Moses and Elijah (4:4), the same ones who will meet with Jesus on the Mount of Transfiguration (Matthew 17).

With the Book of Malachi, we come to the end of the Old Testament. In many translations, the Old Testament ends with the word *curse*. A curse entered the world back in Genesis 3 with the fall of Adam and Eve. But near the end of the New Testament, God tells us that in the new heaven and new earth "there shall be no more curse" (Revelation 22:3). We don't know how many years will have passed, but God will set all things right.

His Coming Unannounced
The study of prophecy is a wonderful thing. It's what first got me interested in the Bible as a young woman, and that study eventually brought me to faith. But it's also a dangerous thing. To spend all your time on it, trying to match it to today's headlines, while neglecting the rest of the Bible is not what God intended.

Prophecy has a divine purpose. Jesus said that He would share things with His friends and He has called us friends. There are a lot of frightening things in prophecy, but we've read the whole Bible and we know how the story ends. Peter, after he described the disappearance of the heavens and the melting down of earth (when God re-creates them), asks the question, "What kind of people ought you to be?" Then he answers his own question: "You ought to live holy and godly lives as you look forward to the day of God and speed its coming" (2 Peter 3:11–12).

Jesus emphasized to His followers repeatedly that He would come again at a time when the world would not be looking for Him. No one can predict the day or the hour. Jesus compared His coming again to a thief breaking into a house in the night. "But understand this: If the owner of the house had known at what time of night the thief was coming, he would have kept watch and would not have let his house be broken into" (Matthew 24:43).

This was illustrated for me recently when I was with a young woman who told about a lesson she learned as a young teen. One evening she was babysitting her siblings who were about five years younger. Despite the instructions her parents had given her about diligently watching them, she was in her room with the door shut, playing music, and talking on the phone. Because of this, she didn't realize that her parents had come home earlier than expected and realized she wasn't watching the kids.

Her father decided to teach her a lesson. He told his wife to take the younger children away. When they were gone, he left the front door wide open, hid and made a noise that caused the teenager to come out of her room dragging the phone and its cord with her. She dropped the phone, ran to the open door and began calling her siblings. She went out in the yard searching for them. Unable to find them, she returned to the house. As she came through the door, her father snuck up behind her, put his hand over her mouth and lifted her off her feet. She said her heart was in her throat and she was terrified. Then he dropped her. She looked around and saw her father. She didn't go into any more details, but she said after that night she became the best babysitter in the world.

My friend's father had played the part of a thief in the night and dramatically made his point. That story made me think of the coming again of Christ. That promise is a comfort to believers and a danger to unbelievers. He's coming like a thief in the night, and a thief never comes when you're ready for him, sitting with a shotgun across your knees watching the door.

All of us are warned to be watchful: for no one knows when the Son of Man is coming. So be ready. He's coming at an hour you don't expect—like my young friend's father.

And Many More

The Coming Ruler	Micah 5:1–4
The Second David	Hosea 3:4–5
The Rebuilder	Amos 9:11–15
The Branch of the Lord	Isaiah 4:2
Wonderful Counselor	Isaiah 9:1–7
The Reigning Messiah	Isaiah 11:1–16
Triumphant One	Isaiah 24:21–25
The Conqueror	Isaiah 63:1–6
The Priestly King	Jeremiah 30:9, 21
The Rightful King	Ezekiel 21:25–27
Unifier of the Nation	Ezekiel 37:15–28
The Anointed Ruler	Daniel 9:24–27
Desire of Nations	Haggai 2:6–9
God's Signet Ring	Haggai 2:21–23
King-Priest over All	Zechariah 6:9–15
The Entering King	Zechariah 9:9–10
Sun of Righteousness	Malachi 4:2

Chapter 17
The Jesus We Know

My husband and I recently had an anniversary. We didn't need or want anything particular so I suggested we give each other a DNA ancestry test. He found a company, and we sent the cheek swabs off together. His came back first declaring him 97% English-Irish and 3% Middle Eastern. (He is so Anglo that even the 3% was a shock.)

When the company emailed mine a few days later, the colored circles that indicated the lands of my ancestors trailed across the map of the Eastern hemisphere. That was even more of a shock. I had known about Turkish ancestors and my straight-off-the-boat Irish great-grandfather, but my ancestry was more like a League of Nations. Although I am red-headed and look Irish, apparently I am about a third Italian and a quarter Scandinavian. The Scandinavian part had never occurred to me, even though my family tree has a big "Sweeney" branch. The rest of the percentages are a combination of Balkan, Middle Eastern, Southeast Asian (the Indian peninsula)—and a small percentage Ashkenazi (European) Jewish.

My husband decided his ancestry seemed boring compared to my varied roots. Even though the Jewish part is very small, I'm happy to have it. Now he calls me his "Roman Jew." At Easter he said, "I think it's great that you are related to Jesus' earthly people." I do too. And, similar to what the TV commercials for testing ancestry say, it makes me wonder if my lifelong love for the Jewish people and the land of Israel reverberates because of something in my bloodline or comes more from what I've learned in the Bible.

During both my trips to Israel I, like every Christian tourist, wondered if I was walking where Jesus walked. Or could I have been standing where He had stood looking out on the Sea of Galilee? The feeling is more likely in that region than in the streets of Jerusalem because the streets from Jesus' day are underground. The city has been destroyed several times and rebuilt on top of the rubble. Other places have changed drastically because large churches were built on top of a presumed historic site.

Some tourists return from their trip to the Holy Land, glad they went, but admitting to being somewhat disappointed. Their idea of looking for Jesus in the land of His birth had become a spiritualized version of "Where's Waldo?" They hoped (and even prayed) that it would be the catalyst for bringing them closer to Jesus. Particularly, that they would begin to *feel* a closer connection.

I know because I did that. And I was one of the people who came back both times having had a wonderful trip and having seen many great places. But did I feel a lot closer to Jesus? I can't say that I did.

We may go to Israel believing we'll find something to draw us closer to Him. Yet the truth is that when believers travel to Israel, we take Jesus with us. After all, He's the One who promised to never leave us or forsake us. Seeing the land He walked on can help us understand Bible passages more fully, but it isn't what fills our heart. If we don't recognize Him here, we won't find Him there.

A popular song from a couple of decades ago said that God is watching us "from a distance." It was a catchy tune but poor theology. For believers, there is no distance. God is as close as the breath inside you. I've always believed that but was glad to find some proof in Dr. Richard Swenson's book, *More than Meets the Eye*. In it Swenson, a medical doctor, uses his expertise to show the intricacies of God's creation—the human body. One section particularly has influenced the nearness I feel to Jesus:

"Every breath we take contains 150 million molecules that were breathed by Jesus Christ. Yes, that is *every* breath, and 150 million molecules. It is one of the ways He intimately shares life with us. If ever we think we are doing something in secret away from the presence of God, it would probably be fitting to hold our breath while doing so. For whenever we inhale, Jesus is there with us sharing Himself minute by minute and molecule by molecule."

To Know Him

Wanting to know Christ better and to sense His presence more is a natural goal for every Christ follower. But what if there is some impediment in your life—whether some wound in your past or something in your present that blocks you from it? Whenever I start looking at the pain or problems in my life rather than concentrating on the presence of Christ, I think of a woman who had far more difficulties than most: Helen Keller.

Helen Keller's book, *The Story of My Life*, was made into a movie called *The Miracle Worker*, and released in 1962. Shot in black and white, the starkness of the film showcases the gravity of the situation. Anne Bancroft plays Annie Sullivan, the woman who taught a blind, deaf, and mute child how to communicate with the world around her. Patty Duke, in her first major role, plays Helen as a child.

The film is set in the 1880s in Tuscumbia, Alabama, where Helen was born a healthy infant. But when she was 19 months old, a disease—possibly scarlet fever or meningitis—destroyed her sight and hearing. Not able to hear, she also didn't learn to speak.

In the film, we repeatedly see a frustrated and violent Helen, unable to communicate any other way, lash out at everything and everyone. Her parents pity her too much to make her behave. They hire a succession of people to help control her. When she is seven, as a last resort her parents approach the Perkins Institute, an "asylum" for the blind. The school sends them Annie Sullivan, a "half-blind Yankee schoolgirl" who had grown up in the school. Annie had been blind but had some sight restored through a series of operations.

Annie or *Teacher*, as Helen will come to call her, is as headstrong as Helen. She stands up to Helen's autocratic father, and won't accept tantrums from a child. Even a severely handicapped child. She is convinced that, with work, Helen can learn a tactile sign language that will open the world to her. But Helen doesn't want to work. She doesn't understand when Teacher grabs her hand and traces shapes on her palm with her finger. She reacts as if Teacher is trying to restrain her.

The breakthrough comes as Annie drags a fit-throwing Helen to the water pump in the yard to clean her up from a self-made mess. Even then she tries to teach Helen by signing the word "water" into her hands each time water touches them. Suddenly, Helen stops writhing. Her face shows something has happened. She holds her hand out to have it done again. She touches the water. She signs the word back into her teacher's hand. Teacher holds Helen's hand to her face as she nods. "Yes."

We watch Helen joyfully stumble from one object to another, putting out her hand to ask for the word, then spelling it back into her teacher's hand. As Teacher says, now "she knows."

Helen throws her arms around the necks of her parents and accepts the affection they'd so wanted, but weren't able, to give her. Tears run from her sightless eyes. She has been rescued.

There's much more to her story. Helen had a brilliant mind. She learned to speak, even though she couldn't hear her own voice. She graduated from Radcliffe, traveled to 39 countries, lectured before thousands, and wrote 13 books. All because one woman understood her distress and persisted until she opened a whole new world to Helen.

Helen Keller's life was radically changed. If Annie Sullivan had not intervened when she was a child, Helen could have become a bitter woman trapped in a dark, silent world. Instead, she became a world-renowned author and speaker. She also became a Christian.

Sometime after she learned to communicate through signing, Helen was told about Jesus and how He gave His life for all who would come to Him. Her answer shows that He still reaches into the darkest places in hearts and minds.

She said, "I knew Him. I knew Him. I just didn't know His name."

Without a Doubt

I started this book telling you how I learned about Jesus when I was a child but didn't come to truly know Him until I was an adult. Your story may be very different. While many have a dramatic conversion experience that radically changes their lives, some experience ups and downs in their faith-life. And those ups and downs can cause them to doubt that their conversion was real.

My son Cole was 15 and at a Christian summer camp when He surrendered his life to the ministry. He grew in his faith and our pastor allowed him to preach several times. When Cole was 18, a father-son evangelist team held a revival at our church. We soon discovered their methodology was to stir the emotions of the teenagers in the church and get all of them to doubt whether they were *actually* saved. This made for several dramatic scenes at the altar but caused real damage in the youth group. The problem was that teenagers we'd all been praying would be converted, weren't. And the teenagers who began doubting their salvation were some of the most obviously saved and dedicated ones—including Cole.

So he and I had a sort of "you've *already* come to Jesus" moment. We went over what he believed and why. Then we looked at 1 John 5:13:

I write these things to you who believe in the name of the Son of God so that you may know that you have eternal life.

I asked him if he believed that verse and he said he did. I asked him to write that day's date next to it and to treat it as a spiritual marker. If he was ever tempted to doubt again, I asked him to go back to that verse and reaffirm what he knew—that he knew Jesus. I don't know if he's ever had to go back to that marker, but since then Cole has spent more than 20 years in full-time ministry as a pastor.

When you look at the subject of doubt logically, having doubts can be a sign that you *are* a believer. The devil isn't dividing his own house trying to get people who aren't believers, but think they are, to doubt the salvation they don't really have. If they did, they might wake up and actually become believers. It's believers that he tries to confuse. Whenever a doubt crosses my mind—and doubts do cross all our minds at times—I pray what the father of a demon-possessed boy begged of Jesus in Mark 9:24 (NKJV): "Lord, I believe; help my unbelief!"

Think of the person closest to you—the one you know best—whether your spouse, parent, child, lifelong best friend. Could anyone convince you that the depth of that relationship is a figment of your imagination? The best antidote for doubt is to get to know Jesus better. When you walk and talk with Jesus, when you see Him revealed in His Word, when He becomes as real to you as the person you know best, the doubts pretty much go away.

In this book we've followed Jesus—the pre-incarnate Christ—through many of His appearances in the Old Testament:

He created all things. He walked with Adam and Eve in the Garden. He ate with Abraham. He talked with Moses. He led the children of Israel through the wilderness. He commanded their army. He inspired the sweet singer of Israel. He was the coming Messiah the prophets pondered.

In type He was pictured: as a ram and a lamb, fire and water, a cloud of glory and the sun of righteousness, the king-priest, the son to be sacrificed, and much more. He was all this before He was the baby born in Bethlehem and the Savior who died on Calvary.

Do you know Him? He wants a deeper relationship with you—more than you can possibly imagine. He died to provide it.

As we close, this is my prayer for you:

That you *know* that you know Jesus,
That you come to know Him better day by day,
And that you grow in grace and knowledge of Him.

SOURCES

Barnhouse, Donald G., *Genesis*, Zondervan, Grand Rapids, MI, 1973.

Baxter, G. Sidlow, *Explore the Book*, Zondervan, Grand Rapids, MI, 1960.

Geisler, Norman, *A Popular Survey of the Old Testament*, Hendrickson Publishers, Peabody, MA, 1977.

Guthrie, Nancy, *Seeing Jesus in the Old Testament* (a series of five books), Crossway Books, Wheaton, IL, 2011-2014.

Kaiser, Jr., Walt, *The Messiah in the Old Testament*, Zondervan, Grand Rapids, MI, 1995.

Peterson, Eugene, *The Jesus Way*, Eerdmans, Grand Rapids, MI, 2007.

Roper, David, *Jacob: The Fools God Chooses*, Discovery House Publishers, Grand Rapids, MI, 2002.

Swenson, Dr. Richard, *More than Meets the Eye*, NavPress, Colorado Springs, CO, 2000.

Swindoll, Charles, *Abraham*, Tyndale House, Carol Stream, IL, 2014.

Swindoll, Charles, *Moses: A Man of Selfless Dedication*, Word, Nashville, TN, 1999.

Wiersbe, Warren, *The Wiersbe Bible Commentary*, Victor Books, Colorado Springs, CO, 2007.

Made in the USA
Coppell, TX
23 December 2020